At last, Barbara Wendland has written the book for which we have all been waiting! In her easy-to-read but thoughtful style, and informed by thousands of church "misfits" with whom she has communicated through her monthly newsletter *Connections*, Barbara has put into words, with courage, candor, compassion and conviction, what so many have long thought in silence. She assures us that we are not alone, that our questions are both valid and vital, and that we need to speak out boldly when churches strive to preserve an outdated, exclusive or harmful status quo. Every person occupying a church pew—and all who have left—should read this excellent book.

—Dr. Val Webb, theologian and author of *Stepping out with
the Sacred: Human Attempts to Engage the Divine.*

Barbara Wendland's keen ability to connect books read and life lived has created a reference text for those of us who've been living secretly as "misfits." She lays out a provocative process for transforming our anonymous misfit experiences into bottom-up institutional change, whether in the church or in the communities we live in."

—David Dykes, D.L. Dykes, Jr. Foundation, Faith and Reason

Barbara Wendland has been one of the church's most eloquent and persistent spokespersons for a renewed vision of what our religious and spiritual life might be. Her view is always thoughtful, prayerful, inclusive, generous, and determined to serve the world as Jesus intended. The story of how she arrived at this place is deeply compelling and important to the church, whatever the denomination —and immensely reassuring to those of us who have been dwelling at the margins as "misfits."

—Gary Holthaus, author of *The Unauthorized Bible*
and *Learning Native Wisdom*

In a climate where the basic message of church and religion is to fit in and to adjust to the powers that be, *Misfits* sets out to turn the tables. The future of the church is tied up with the following questions: What if the true nature of church is found in the margins, with those who push beyond its current domestication? What if those who raise questions are more faithful than those who always nod in agreement? The lives of Jesus and the prophets testify to the importance of misfits and, as Barbara Wendland rightly notes, "following Jesus means being a misfit."

—Joerg Rieger, Wendland-Cook Professor of Constructive Theology,
Perkins School of Theology, Southern Methodist University

Misfits

The Church's Hidden Strength

BARBARA WENDLAND

St. Johann Press
Haworth, New Jersey

ST. JOHANN PRESS

Published in the United States of America
by St. Johann Press
P.O. Box 241
Haworth, NJ 07641
www.stjohannpress.com

Copyright © 2010 Barbara Wendland

The paper used in this publication meets the minimum require-
ments of the American National Standard for Information
Sciences—Permanence of Paper for Printed Library Materials,
ANSI/NISO Z39/48-1992

Interior design and composition by Susan Ramondo
(susan@srdesktopservices.com)

Cover design: G&H SOHO, Inc.
www.ghsoho.com

ISBN 978-1-878282-66-8

Manufactured in the United States of America

Contents

Introduction

Hearing Misfits' Cries

"I thought I must be the only one who felt this way."

"I'm so glad to know I'm not alone!"

"I was afraid something was wrong with me."

Comments like these are the most frequent responses I get from readers of *Connections*, my monthly letter urging the church to reexamine its beliefs, speak today's language, and openly address today's most important topics. The people who send me these comments are Christians. Many are well-informed about the Bible, theology, church history, and related subjects. Many are lifelong churchgoers, like me. Yet surprisingly many of us feel like outsiders in our own churches—ignored, abandoned, sometimes even actively rejected. We feel like misfits. And ironically, we get the impression that what makes us misfits is mainly our efforts to become informed about the Bible, to look realistically at it and at the church, and to follow the teaching and example of Jesus more closely, in the hope of making a difference in the world.

Why do so many of us who want so much to make a difference feel so alone in the church? Even worse, why does the church seem not to care or even notice how we feel? After all, Jesus was a misfit in his world. He was very much a minority voice. How can the church follow him without listening to minority voices?

I'm writing this book because I believe many more Christians need to be asking these questions. Church misfits need to speak out and keep speaking out, even when no one seems to be listening. "Fits" and other church leaders need to recognize that the misfits are not mere troublemakers but are deeply concerned fellow Christians who deserve a voice in the church and a seat at its tables.

Many church misfits have strengths that the church and the world desperately need. But many of those strengths are now being hidden. The church too often ignores or even stifles them.

MANY YEARS OF TRYING TO FIT

Starting to feel like a misfit in the church in recent years came as a surprise to me, because I've been an active church member all my life. I was baptized as a baby. Throughout my childhood, my parents took me to church with them every Sunday. As an adult, I taught Sunday School and Vacation Bible School and other classes for years. I made casseroles for potluck suppers. My husband and I sang in the choir for years. We both served on committees and held offices. We gave regularly to the church budget, mission trips, and building campaigns. I was elected as a delegate to my denomination's top governing body. I've wanted to do whatever I could to help the church succeed. I've tried to promote what I understood to be its God-given calling.

For many of those years, I kept quiet and stayed in the background, conforming to whatever my friends, family, and church seemed to expect. I was trying hard to fit in, and to a great extent I succeeded. But in midlife, I started seeing that pain and even dishonesty had too often been part of silently fitting in. I began to see the needs of the church and the world more clearly. I saw that many of my newly realized concerns made me a misfit but that being a misfit wasn't all bad. In fact, I started seeing that in some ways, following Jesus requires *not* fitting in.

That new awareness made me stop going along quietly. It made me start acknowledging my real questions. Yet the result, especially in the last few years, has been indifference and even disapproval from my church. The more I've learned about the

Bible and church history and structure, and the more I've risked speaking out about issues that seem important to me, the less welcome I've felt in the church, especially in my own congregation. That hurts.

THERE ARE LOTS OF US MISFITS

Even though I've come to feel alone and unwanted in my home congregation, however, I've found I'm far from alone in the wider church. During my eighteen years of writing *Connections*, by far the most responses I've gotten from readers have been to my admissions of feeling like a misfit. And these responses have been grateful and impassioned as well as numerous.

Here's how one layman described his feelings. "Your *Connections* addresses some issues that have troubled me for a long, long time. But until now I was never able to understand what the problem was. I now realize that I am not alone out here. There may be only two of us who feel this way, but I now know there are at least two, and that's one more than I expected."

Actually there are a lot of us, even among very active church-goers. Many of us are not very visible, because we have given up in exhaustion or have lost interest and concluded that speaking up is futile, even if we keep going through the motions of attending church activities.

ENTERING A TIME WARP

We've lost interest especially because so much of what we hear churches and individual Christians saying seems so unrelated to life in today's world. When I enter a typical worship service, I feel like I'm stepping into a time warp. I keep hearing "thee" and "thou" and "wouldst" and "doth" and other seventeenth-century words, even in so-called contemporary services. Creeds, hymns, and prayers contradict well-known facts of human biology. Some portray the earth as flat. And important current issues don't seem to exist. The Iraq and Afghanistan wars, the Israeli-Palestinian conflicts, the debates on immigration and health care and capital punishment and torture—when I'm in church, all these seem to be happening somewhere else, not in our world.

Every time I write in *Connections* about being turned off by this time-warp feeling, I'm reminded again that I'm far from the only turned-off person. "I'm so glad someone is finally speaking up about these things!" readers say, over and over. "I'm a lifelong churchgoer, fifty-one years old," one writes, "but in church I've felt like an alien in a foreign land for the past twenty years."

FEELING UNSUPPORTED

However, the problem isn't just that we misfits lose interest because of seeing the church living in the past instead of the present. That's only the tip of an iceberg. For many of us, a big part of the iceberg is that we're hurting in silence because our churches have rejected us or refused to support our efforts to follow the example set by Jesus.

Those of us struggling against the flow include clergy as well as lay Christians. Here's how one pastor described how it hurts to feel that he's not free to reveal his real beliefs to church members, or to share with them findings about the Bible that have been life-giving for him. "It has become so difficult that I will be taking early retirement from the ministry," he wrote. "If I stay in, I will drown." I understood how he felt. There's a limit to how long anyone can keep swimming upstream.

THE LIFE OF OUR CHURCHES IS AT STAKE

We misfits are pleading to be treated with compassion. Isn't that how Christians are called to treat everyone? But our cries from the wilderness are not only pleas for compassion. They are also warnings that the church's life—its real heart and soul, not just its membership numbers or level of activity—is at stake. We are saying to church members that it is essential, a life-and-death issue, to present broader, more welcoming images of God than those we are now offering. We are reminding the church that it needs to let its members know what the best scholars have learned about the Bible's origin and the earthly life of Jesus. And we are urging the church to stop excluding not only the people whose race, culture, or sexual orientation differs from the majority of church members, but also those whose interpretation of the Bible and understanding of Christianity differ from the majority view.

Our nation and the rest of the world are suffering from violence, widespread poverty, lack of health care, and a deteriorating natural environment. Many of the people who feel like church misfits are able and even eager to help address such issues. Many are visionaries who can offer much-needed ways of seeing beyond "the way we've always done it." But only by bringing the misfits and the churches together can we achieve the results that the world so urgently needs.

ARE WE BRAVE ENOUGH?

As a first step, the church must hear the cries of the misfits. It must notice how they're hurting and how they could help the church and the world. Then it must stop driving them off and find ways to welcome them instead. It must let their hidden strengths come out of hiding.

Making these changes would mean taking some risks but also reaping some benefits. It could cause our churches to lose some members, because some apparently like having a time warp to escape into. But changing could lead the church to following Jesus more closely. It would probably help add some members, too—people who have been avoiding the church because they see it as out of touch with reality and even with the Jesus it claims to follow. So the crucial question is whether we're brave enough to risk bringing the misfits out into the open in the church and making some of the changes they recognize the need for.

THE RESULTS CAN BE REWARDING

As I've started openly admitting my own misfit views and concerns in the past several years, I've seen firsthand how much that openness can sometimes cost. I've seen that some church members feel that people with views like mine shouldn't be allowed a voice in the church. Some say my views show that I'm not a Christian. Many say that being a Christian requires believing all the beliefs and doctrines and following all the religious practices that are seen as essential by most churchgoers today and are officially prescribed by the institutional church. But I disagree. I don't think acceptance by the majority proves a belief correct or means a practice is a requirement for being Christian. Official adoption by the institutional church doesn't do that, either. What is required of Christians instead is to see the practice of compassion, justice, and nonviolence as one's goal and to actively work toward that goal. It's to make Jesus, not the majority, one's guide.

Despite having experienced rejection by my church, I've seen how rewarding the results of openly admitting one's real beliefs and concerns can be. I've also seen how great the need for change is in the church. So even if you're skeptical so far, I hope you'll keep reading.

The message I'm sharing here may be most important for people who don't feel like church misfits. If you're a "fit," you have power that we misfits lack. You can help both the misfits and the church by helping to make the misfits' strengths more available to the church. As you read my story and my plea, I hope you'll consider doing that.

I

Keeping Quiet, Trying to Fit

FOR THE FIRST FORTY years of my life I was a quiet, docile, stay-in-the-background, do-what-you're-told, don't-even-ask-questions conformist. I functioned this way not only in the church but also in every other aspect of my life. I now know that at heart I was a misfit all along in some ways, but for many years I thought fitting in was the only right thing to do, so I did it.

I'd like to tell you what led me to change. Why? For essentially the same reason author Frederick Buechner gives for telling his story, in his book *Telling Secrets*. "Who cares?" he asks himself. "What in the world could be less important than who I am and who my father and mother were, the mistakes I have made . . . , the occasional discoveries, the bad times and the good times, the moments of grace . . ." Then he answers his own question. "My story is important not because it is mine, God knows, but because if I tell it anything like right, the chances are that you will recognize that in many ways it is also yours."[1]

If you see similarities between my story and yours, I hope they will help you see that change is possible for you just as it has turned out to be for me. I hope you'll see, too, that some changes

---

[1]Frederick Buechner. *Telling Secrets: A Memoir* (New York: HarperSanFrancisco, 1991), 29–30.

1

could make your life more satisfying for you and others around you. And who knows—your changing might also help revitalize the church. It could even help change the world.

But even if my story doesn't seem similar to yours, you may still find reading mine helpful. It could help you see why other Christians' interpretations of the Bible or expectations of the church differ from yours, and why that doesn't necessarily mean they're wrong. So if you see anything you think the church needs to learn from, in my story or in what I report from the stories of others, I hope you'll speak up in the church about what you see.

A CHURCH EXPERIENCE THAT MISSED THE MARK

I grew up in Houston as the only child of loving, conservative parents. My parents and grandparents were all active, churchgoing Methodists so I automatically became one too. I was baptized as a baby. Then when I was in the fourth grade I joined the church along with everyone else in my Sunday School class. In my denomination that step is now called confirmation and usually seems to happen when children are a little older, but in my childhood congregation it was standard operating procedure for fourth-graders. It didn't involve any real decision, as far as I could tell. It was simply what everyone was expected to do.

All of us fourth-graders had to attend a preparation class weekly for several weeks before joining the church. The class met in the chapel of our big, Gothic-cathedral-style church building. The chapel, like the sanctuary, had dark stained-glass windows, dark wood, and maroon velveteen cushions on the pews. The building was beautiful but also a bit eerie to me, especially when it was mostly empty, as it always was when my confirmation class met.

During the weeks of the class, each child had to meet individually with our senior pastor in his office, and I dreaded having to do that. His office was on the third floor of the building, and I was uneasy about having to go there alone. It felt scary.

Besides, the pastor seemed forbidding to me. He had steel-gray hair and always wore a black suit. Sometimes he had a simpery smile, but otherwise I never saw any sign of life from him. For me his sermons were a chore to sit through, and I had little other contact with him. To me, he seemed like just one more piece of the sanctuary furniture. Fortunately, though, our class time ran out before each of us had a chance to meet with him. I got to go in a group of leftovers instead of having to go alone. That let me stay silently in the background instead of saying anything to him or having him say anything to me.

On the Sunday morning when my classmates and I joined the church, I was ready before my mother was, so I stood by her dresser talking to her while she finished doing her makeup and hair. I picked up her lipstick and opened it, and it fell down the front of my new pale pink dress. Mama's frantic efforts with spot remover couldn't get quite all of the red streak out, and having to stop and work on it made us late getting to the church. I don't remember anything about the actual confirmation service. I only remember that the morning was not a happy one.

I COULDN'T MAKE THE VOWS NOW

The church treats the step of making a formal public commitment to Jesus Christ and to the church—baptism for adults or confirmation for those who have been baptized as infants—as essential for being a Christian. It is expected to have a lifelong positive impact. For me, however, the unpleasant aspects of my confirmation—the forbidding pastor, the scary building, and my routine-disrupting accident—obscured whatever spiritual significance it was meant to have. I wonder how many other members—fits as well as misfits— also find that superficial conditions hide the intended value of such church practices for them.

More important, I wonder now about the beliefs that confirmation and baptismal vows affirm. When I hear the vows being given to new members now, I know that I could not honestly make those vows now, because of how my understanding has changed. In fact, I now doubt that the church's expectation—implied, if not stated—of lifelong commitment to such vows is reasonable, especially if they're made early in life. That expectation denies that the Holy Spirit will keep speaking to us throughout our lives, bringing us new insight and nudging us to keep growing.

If we grow, our beliefs are likely to change. In fact, they will need to change to some extent. At the very least, we may realize that the words of historic baptismal or confirmation vows can't all be taken literally. We're likely to realize that if we're to stay committed to them, their meaning for us must become much broader and deeper than what we originally saw.

DUTIFUL YEARS

For many years after my confirmation, I kept dutifully going to Sunday School and worship and Vacation Bible School and church camp and Methodist Youth Fellowship (MYF) regularly. But the official vows I had made weren't my motivation. Neither was any feeling of having been "converted" or "born again." Like the motivation of many other lifelong churchgoers, mine came mostly from habit and the expectations of my family and everyone else I knew.

Most of my Sunday School classes were far from inspiring. They met in rooms that were painted institutional-green and had bookshelves filled with yellowing, outdated lesson materials. Most of the classes were led by older women who overused the word "meaningful" and wore dark crepe dresses and "sensible shoes." (These women probably weren't as old as I am now, and their shoes no more clunky than those I now wear!) These women undoubtedly were strongly committed Christians. But because their appearance and manner were so unattractive to me and so different from all the other women I knew (because they were misfits, that is, though not in the ways I now see as valuable for Christians), they were a big turnoff for me.

So was a lot of the music. I still remember one of those dreary women playing MacDowell's "To a Wild Rose" on the piano every morning at the start of Vacation Bible School. She said the piece created a "meaningful atmosphere," but it gave me a creepy feeling and still revives that feeling whenever I hear it. With sweetly pious facial expressions and eyes cast skyward, in swooping voices these ever-present women led us regularly in singing "Sweet Hour of Prayer" and other equally syrupy hymns.

These well-meaning women certainly didn't encourage questions or differences of opinion. Some didn't even allow such things. A longtime friend reminded me only recently of an experience she had in our Sunday School class during our high-school years. She had dared to say that she couldn't believe that God was like an old man in the sky with a white beard, which was the picture she got from the church. Our teacher was appalled. That afternoon, she phoned my friend's mother to report what her daughter had said in class, obviously expecting the mother to punish her daughter or at least order her never to do such a thing again.

WHAT'S PROFANE? WHAT'S SACRED?

These women enforced the church rules, too, many of which were apparently aimed at preventing activities that were considered profane in places that were considered sacred. During my high-school years, we teenagers weren't allowed to have dances in the church gym because it was in the same building as the sanctuary. That never made sense to me. Evidently if the gym had been in a separate building, dancing in it would have been okay.

I remember being ousted from the church's chapel for practicing the Cole Porter song "Night and Day" on its piano with a fellow MYF member. She and I were to perform the duet the next day at school, and the time between two church meetings, when the building was mostly empty, seemed to us like the ideal opportunity for our last-minute practice. But a church staff member rushed in and made us stop when she heard us. Years later, my thoughts went back to that experience when I first read the statement by Jesuit priest Pierre Teilhard de Chardin that is still one of my favorites: ". . . *nothing* here below is *profane* for those who know how to see."[2]

Good friends and some good times came from those years in the church, yet those weren't my reason for going to church. Instead, I went because I knew that I was supposed to do what my family and friends considered proper, and to believe what they apparently believed. Unfortunately, a big part of what I learned from those years in church was that dullness, surface sweetness, and unquestioning conformity—following all rules and obeying all authorities—were what being Christian required. Now, I know that that impression of Christianity was mistaken. These characteristics often reveal *failure* to follow the way of Jesus.

A COMPELLING BUT UNNERVING EXPERIENCE

An important exception to the uninspiring impression I got from most church leaders and activities during those years was the Youth Week that happened every summer during my teenage years. It always featured a guest speaker and included picnics and swimming parties that were a welcome change from routine MYF activities. I'll never forget the closing worship service of one of those weeks. It was in our imposing church sanctuary. The lights were low except above the altar and pulpit. The lighted stained-glass picture high above the altar, of Jesus praying in Gethsemane, was a focal point. The guest speaker was a dynamic young pastor, a striking and welcome contrast to the bland older men who were always my congregation's senior pastors. His sermon that night was powerful and dramatic. It was based on Isaiah 6:8, the scripture that had been the week's theme: "Whom shall we send, and who will go for us? Here am I. Send me." At the end, he

---

[2]Pierre Teilhard de Chardin, *The Divine Milieu* (New York: Harper & Row, 1960), 66.

asked all of us who were willing to commit our lives to Christ to come forward to the altar as the organ played the hymn "O Jesus, I Have Promised."

I assumed everyone would go forward. Whatever he had said had sounded to me like what everyone was supposed to do, so in my usual do-whatever-I'm-supposed-to-do way, I went forward. But to my dismay, I was alone except for a couple of church staff members. I wanted to drop through the floor.

"NO, NO! I DIDN'T MEAN IT!"

Afterward, several staff members rushed up and congratulated me on having made a commitment to "full-time Christian service." I was shocked and scared. That wasn't what I meant at all! What had I really done, I wondered. What if God was going to hold me accountable for what I had promised without intending it? I wanted to shout to God and everyone, "No, no! I didn't mean it!"

When that Youth Week ended, I lost track of the inspiring pastor who spoke, but in recent years I rediscovered him. He's nearing ninety now and has recently retired for the second time, and he's still as powerful a speaker as ever. He's one of my favorite kindred spirits, and he writes me often to encourage me in what I'm now doing.

My other remnant of that Youth Week experience is that when I hear "O Jesus, I Have Promised," I still get a little uneasy and wonder what I really committed to. Maybe what I did was valid, even though not in the way the church staff members interpreted it. In those years, what church people meant when they talked about full-time Christian service was being a pastor if you were male, or a missionary or Director of Christian Education if you were female, and I was quite sure those occupations weren't for me. I'm still quite sure of that, but I have a different understanding of full-time Christian service now. I think it's what every Christian is meant to do, though for most it doesn't mean being a pastor or a missionary or any other kind of church professional. Instead, I now believe, it means being compassionate and actively promoting justice in the course of whatever one's daily work may be. Maybe I understood that at some level when I went forward that night.

OBLIVIOUS TO THE WIDER WORLD

During those growing-up years, I essentially wore blinders with regard to everything beyond my circle of friends and family. I was oblivious to the injustice of common practices like racial segregation, for example. The people now called African-American were then called Negroes or the n-word that is now taboo, by everyone I knew. The only Negroes I knew were my family's occasional maid and her husband, our yardman. My parents and I called them only by their first names, of course, not Mr. and Mrs. They lived far across Houston from us, and when Mama occasionally took one of them home, he or she sat in the back seat of our car, even when the front passenger seat was empty. I often rode the city buses to downtown Houston for shopping or going to the library or dentist, and Negroes sat only in the back. Of course they didn't use the same public rest rooms or water fountains or restaurants that we used, and they had their own schools and churches. It never occurred to me that there was anything wrong with this system. It was simply the way things were, and thus, I assumed, the way things were supposed to be.

I didn't know homosexuality existed. I remember two men who attended my church regularly and sat near my parents and me. They always came together, which seemed vaguely unusual to me, because all the other churchgoers seemed to be married couples and their children, but I never gave that difference any real thought.

Also, I gave little thought to world events during those years. There was no TV. We got the local newspaper every day and often listened to the radio in the evenings, but I didn't pay much attention to news reports. I was vaguely aware of Mahatma Gandhi from seeing him in the newsreels that movie theaters showed before every movie. But he was in a strange, faraway place and was so strange-looking, so strangely dressed, and he was a follower of some strange religion. I knew only that he was a troublemaker who was always fasting and getting his followers to riot. I had no idea why. I just knew those were bad things to do.

Later as a young adult, I was of course aware of Martin Luther King, Jr. But the comments I heard about him from everyone I knew assured me that he too was a reprehensible troublemaker. He was breaking laws and customs and disrupting the lives of law-abiding people, so he obviously needed to be stopped. And the changes he wanted, letting black people eat in white restaurants, go to white schools, and sit by white people on buses, were unthinkable.

"YOU'RE NOT GOING TO BE AN ENGINEER, ARE YOU!"

Like not noticing anything wrong with the racial segregation I lived in the midst of, for a long time I didn't notice anything wrong with how women were kept in second-class roles. Eventually, as a young adult, I had occasional vague misgivings about it, but even then, I assumed it was the way things were supposed to be. Only at midlife did I finally start seeing clearly and admitting to myself that something about that system was seriously wrong.

One shocking confirmation of the system's wrongness came in my fifties when I was going through my mother's mementos after her death and found a standardized test she'd saved. A cousin who was a public-school teacher had given it to me for fun before I started to school. Here's a sentence from a part that tested the student's reading ability: "Fathers are strong and good." Nothing about mothers being strong and good too. And here's another: "Girls belong at home." Amazing. It was blatant brainwashing.

I loved school and always did well in it, but in the eighth grade I ran into trouble. All students had to submit four-year plans for their coming high school years, in preparation for college. I had no idea what my college major might turn out to be, because I didn't really know what I might be interested in. I just did what I was supposed to do. I didn't think what I *wanted* to do mattered very much. So I filled my proposed schedule with four years of English, four of math, four of foreign language, and four of science, to prepare for whatever might come later. Then I took my plan to the school counselor whose approval was required. My school was large, so I'd never seen her before and she'd never seen me. She was appalled. She immediately started erasing. She said this was too heavy a schedule for anyone. She said I must take a study hall each year instead of one of the subjects I had listed. When I objected (a rare move for me then), she relented enough to leave everything except solid geometry, which she replaced with chorus. "You're *certainly* never going to need solid geometry!" she said with a sneer. "*You're* not going to be an *engineer*, are you?" I had no idea what engineers did, but I knew that they were male and I wasn't, so I meekly said no and gave up. I enjoyed the chorus class, which introduced me to Gilbert and Sullivan operettas, but years later when I was majoring in math in college, I wished for that solid geometry that I could so easily have taken in high school.

HEARING UNBELIEVABLE THINGS IN CHURCH

In my early years the mistreatment of black people or women didn't raise any questions in my mind, but some of what I heard regularly in church did. I never questioned it out loud, because no one else was questioning it and I certainly wasn't willing to be the only one. But I wondered about a lot of things.

The scriptures that described God speaking to people through dreams made me wonder. In sermons and Sunday School classes I often heard the story of Joseph interpreting Pharaoh's dreams (Genesis 41:1–36). I heard about God speaking to Jacob through his dream of a ladder (Genesis 28:10–17). I heard about Joseph, the father of Jesus, being warned by God in a dream not to go back home because Herod was having babies killed (Matthew 2:13). But none of this matched what I saw as real life. I didn't know anyone who took dreams seriously, and I certainly never heard anyone calling them messages from God. Yet in church we often heard scriptures about dreams being messages from God, and I never heard anyone say, "This is odd. It doesn't make sense."

I wondered, too, about scriptures like the one that says if you have two coats and you see someone who has none, give that person one of yours (Luke 3:11). I always had several coats, and so did everyone I knew, yet they were all churchgoing Christians and I never saw any of them feeling the need to give away all but one of their coats. But I never heard anyone ask, either, "Why are we hearing this scripture presented as if it were an instruction from God, and yet not feeling any need to obey it?" All these things made no sense to me, yet I never heard anyone questioning them or even hinting that they didn't make sense.

AN UNCONVINCING EXPLANATION

Once in a great while, I spoke up at home about something like this or about a custom that to me seemed unnecessary, and my mother always reminded me of what my problem was. "When you get older," she would say sweetly, "you will see why this is right." I knew she was always right about everything, so I thought, "Oh, of course. I guess I will."

Amazingly, I didn't catch on to what was wrong with accepting her explanation, until I was fifty and she was eighty and she said it to me about some familiar belief or custom that I had rather mildly objected to. But by then, I'd already started changing some of my unquestioning-conformist ways. Until then, I just stowed my concerns away in the back of my mind and hoped they would make sense later. And I thought that was the end of it. I didn't know they would stay in my mind for the next twenty or thirty years and then rise up and demand attention.

THE ROLE PRESCRIBED FOR WOMEN

Until then, I covered them up with the busyness of doing what I thought all adult women were supposed to do. I have a degree in math, and after college graduation I had a fascinating job as a mathematician for a few years, doing computer programming in the geophysics research department of a large oil company. But when I married I quit my job. I loved it, and it had great potential, especially since I was one of very few women in such jobs and computers were just coming into general use, but I never thought of it as a career. I knew all along that it was only a time-filler until I married and embarked on what I thought was the only right role for grown women: being a full-time wife, mother, and volunteer doer of the church and community jobs that everyone wanted done but weren't important enough for men to do.

In the church part of that role, I made casseroles for dinners and cookies for teas. I taught second-grade Sunday School and Vacation Bible School. I enlisted other volunteer teachers and planned children's classes. I diligently did the home and community parts of what I saw as the required women's role, too—doing routine household chores regularly, helping at my daughter's schools in various ways, playing the expected wife's role in my husband's professional and civic activities, and helping with the projects and holding the offices of various local organizations, mostly the kind of groups that were only for women.

Once in a while I had an inkling that there was something wrong with limiting women to these roles. It didn't seem right to me for all women to have to do the same thing no matter how different their abilities and interests might be. But I knew that was how it was. Like the many other things that I vaguely wondered about but couldn't see any way to make sense of, and thought I had to conform to whether they made sense or not, I banished that one to the back of my mind and dutifully did what I knew I was supposed to do. And I enjoyed a lot of it.

TWO SURPRISES

A few experiences made me wonder about that pattern of automatically accepting whatever family, friends, and church told me. But because these question-raising experiences happened so rarely, I pushed them to the back of my mind where I'd stowed all the other wonderings that I hadn't known what else to do with.

One such experience happened when I was teaching second-grade Sunday School. One child in my class attended rarely and was very quiet and reticent when she attended. But one Sunday morning she started talking to me the minute she entered the room. Throughout the class period she stuck close to me, touching and talking constantly. I couldn't imagine why. But during the following week, her mother unexpectedly died. I spent the next week taking her with me to Vacation Bible School, helping her talk about her feelings in class, and helping her father give a birthday party for her. I felt that somehow I had been placed in her life at exactly the right time to serve a much-needed purpose. Nothing like that had ever happened to me before.

An attention-getting experience of a different kind was my discovery of a controversial book. I was part of a group in my church that discussed the much-talked-about new book *Situation Ethics*, by Joseph Fletcher (the kind of book that unfortunately would now be considered heretical or at least too controversial for discussion in my congregation). Most group members said how shockingly immoral they thought the book was. It said there could be times when a rule from the Bible needed to be ignored, such as when lying would save an innocent person's life. "What is sometimes good may at other times be evil," Fletcher observed, "and what is sometimes wrong may sometimes be right when it serves a good enough end—*depending on the situation*."[3] It seemed to me that he was advocating the very principle that Jesus taught

---

[3]Joseph Fletcher. *Situation Ethics: The New Morality* (Louisville: Westminster John Knox Press, 1966), 123.

and practiced: doing whatever was compassionate in the situation at hand, instead of merely following a list of rules. We see Jesus acting on this principle, for example, in the story of his healing a man on the Sabbath in violation of a rule (Mark 3:1-4). But the discussion-group members said following this policy would mean that people could just do whatever they felt like doing, which obviously would be immoral. I was pretty sure that wasn't right, but I didn't dare to say so. I was still assuming that when I saw things differently from everyone around me, I must be wrong. Yet I kept having the nagging feeling that I wasn't.

The insight that Fletcher's book gave me was so far from my previous way of thinking (actually, my way of *not* thinking) that for several years I couldn't fully accept it. But that book started making me see that Christianity was more about principles than rules. It started making sense of things in the Bible that had never made sense to me before.

TIME TO START BLOSSOMING

For several years, all I did with experiences like these was to keep them stored away in my mind. Only when turmoil suddenly arose in my church congregation did a lot of my mentally-stored-away things become impossible to ignore. I started to realize that when we notice that a rule or a Bible interpretation or a custom doesn't seem to add up, that awareness often turns out to be the voice of God telling us to stop and think and ask some questions. Admitting to ourselves that something doesn't really make sense is often the first step toward responding to God.

That admission started making a dent in my pattern of keeping quiet and conforming. Here's how Cuban-French author Anaïs Nin describes the point I was steadily approaching: "The time came when the risk it took to remain tight in a bud was more painful than the risk it took to blossom."

II

Waking Up, Speaking Out

IT'S NEVER TOO LATE to wake up and change your thinking.
I didn't start doing it until midlife. That was a lot better than
never doing it, but I hope my story will encourage some readers
not to wait so long.

Turmoil in my local church congregation was my wake-up
call. The cause of the turmoil doesn't matter here, but the result was
that church attendance plummeted. Many members dropped out.
Some of those joined other churches. Others stopped attending
any church. Many who kept attending were angry, including my
husband and me. But we were determined to stay. He had been
in this very congregation for his entire life, and I'd been in it for
the years since our marriage, and we were in it for the long run.
We weren't going to let problems we saw as temporary drive us
away.

But the turmoil made me start wondering some things.
What was the real purpose of the church meant to be? Why did
we do so many things that seemed unlikely to accomplish any
worthwhile purpose, like having potluck dinners? And why were
some new staff members at our church promoting liberal views?
I knew such views were wrong, because all my family members
and friends had always said they were. I got so frustrated with the
situation that I decided I had to investigate these questions.

15

All my life I'd been an avid reader. But for the first several years of my married life, my town had no bookstore and only a small library, so whenever I was in a large city I browsed in bookstores and bought a few books that looked interesting. Some happened to be by famous theologians, including Paul Tillich and Pierre Teilhard de Chardin. I found what these authors said intriguing. However, I suspected they didn't go to church and Sunday School, because they described God and interpreted familiar Bible passages in ways that differed from what I'd always heard. I knew they would be misfits in the churches I was familiar with. But unlike what I heard in church, a lot of what these authors were saying was fascinating to me. It made me think, and much of it made more sense to me than what I typically heard at church. I began to suspect that with regard to the church I might be something of a misfit too. But I knew that was an unacceptable thing to be, so I pushed the possibility to the back of my mind.

The more I read, however, the more I began suspecting that I should take seriously some of the statements I had at first found disturbing. I saw that some behaviors that I had considered unacceptable might actually be admirable, and that some beliefs I had assumed were false were likely to be true. I eventually saw that continuing to fit in, by clinging to all my present beliefs and my family and friends' views, could even be a way of resisting God's nudges toward change.

I kept reading, but I always felt a little guilty about reading for mere enjoyment when there were household jobs like dusting or running the vacuum cleaner that needed doing, as there always were. Besides, I didn't know anyone who read the kinds of things I was reading. In that way, I was definitely a misfit, or at least an oddity, among my friends and family. I therefore suspected that I shouldn't "waste time" on such things. But when the trouble arose in my church, reading became my way of investigating what the church's real purpose was supposed to be.

A MYSTERIOUS COURSE OF STUDY

I re-read the Bible first, then moved on to other books. To my surprise I discovered some written by lay Christians who, like me, weren't church employees but were giving the church a lot of serious thought.

Episcopal layman Keith Miller was the first of those eye-opening authors. His parts of the book *The Edge of Adventure* startled me, especially those in which he acknowledged seeing differences between being a Christian and merely being active in a church. "For many years I had been inwardly sick of the church's programs," Miller daringly admitted, "but I had also supported these programs." He also revealed his observation that "we were a *lot* more clear about our economic orientations than our theological ones."[4] (Looking back at this quote now, I realize that by "our economic orientations" Miller only meant how to raise money for church buildings and other parts of the status quo. I still agree with that aspect of what he was saying, but I now notice that many churches don't seem at all clear about their economic orientations that relate to recognizing economic injustice in society. When I first read *The Edge of Adventure*, my eyes hadn't been opened far enough to see that.)

"I knew that the meaning and purpose I had longed for were real and must be available to other people, because I was finding them," wrote Miller, ". . . but in the organizational life of the church, no one seemed to see that there was even anything wrong."[5]

The church leaders he knew, Miller continued, "seemed to be operating with the strangely blind assumption that [lay members] already have the kind of motivation to risk vulnerable involvement in the world."[6]

---

[4]Keith Miller and Bruce Larson. *The Edge of Adventure: An Experiment in Faith.* (Waco, TX: Word Books, 1974), 143.
[5]Miller and Larson, 144–145.
[6]Miller and Larson, 147.

"We have assumed," he observed, "that a [person's] presence at vestry or deacons' meetings indicates a deep personal commitment to God and [God's] purposes."[7]

When I read statements like these, I felt I'd found a kindred spirit! I realized to my great surprise that I wasn't the only church member who thought the kinds of things I was thinking and wondered about the kinds of things I wondered about. What surprised me most was that a lay church member was daring to speak publicly about them.

Looking for answers to my questions about the church's purpose, I kept discovering more interesting books, and each one led to another. I would read voraciously on one subject, and as soon as I started feeling saturated with it, I'd start wanting to know about a related subject. Then I'd start coming across books on that new subject. Some of these were subjects I'd never previously known much about, hadn't had any desire to know about, or hadn't even been aware of—pentecostalism, for example, and the "documentary hypothesis" about how the Old Testament developed. I began feeling that I was somehow being led through a custom-designed course of study that was preparing me for something, but I had no idea what the something might be.

LEARNING ABOUT MYSELF AND OTHERS

In this constantly growing chain of subjects, I gradually moved from reading about religion, theology, the Bible, and the church, to reading about how to know myself and other people better. I read about typical stages of life, especially midlife, which is where I was then, and about the nudges and opportunities for change it often brings. I became aware, too, of personality types and stages of faith. All of this made me start looking at my habitual ways of functioning. I realized that in many ways I was still acting like a child instead of like an adult.

---

[7]Miller and Larson, 151.

I also became aware of the symbolic language that appears throughout human history and in every culture. It shows up in the sacred documents of all religions, I found, in ways like the Bible's use of the turbulent ocean waters to symbolize the chaos and nothingness that early people imagined as existing before the rest of creation appeared. That discovery gave me another helpful new way of understanding some of the Bible's contents that hadn't made sense before.

Starting to understand symbolic language showed me new meaning in familiar church rituals, too. I gradually noticed that Communion reflected the widespread symbolic use of blood to represent life. It also reflected the common symbolic use of a person's body to represent the person's whole self. I started feeling that when we show Jesus saying, "This is my body, given for you and for many," and "This is my blood," and "Do this in remembrance of me," we're not just being reminded of an event in his earthly life. Instead, or additionally, we're hearing him say, "Give your life, as I have given mine. Give your whole self, as I have given mine. To follow me, do this." Recognizing that deeper, broader, and stronger message in Communion gave it meaning for me that its routine presentation in worship services had never made apparent.

Besides becoming newly aware of the symbolic language spoken by familiar religious rituals, I started seeing how this same symbolic, picture-story language appears also in visual arts, literature, and—to my surprise—dreams. I started seeing how the people, objects, and happenings in dreams could be portraying parts of myself and my ways of functioning. I saw that in this way dreams could be giving me messages that would help me grow if I paid attention to them. Soon afterward, I woke one morning remembering the most powerful dream of my life.

A HEN THAT GAVE BIRTH TO A DUCK

The dream followed a painful day spent at my parents' home. I'd been telling them about the fascinating things I'd been reading.

Until then, I'd mostly been careful not to say anything to my parents that I thought they'd disagree with, or to reveal any behavior that I knew they would disapprove of. But we'd always been close, so I naively thought they'd be as thrilled as I was about all that I was now discovering. My mother was an avid reader who liked learning new things, so I had loaned her one of the books I'd read about personality types. Now I mentioned having learned that I was a different personality type from her and my father, and I commented on how helpful that discovery had been. She was not thrilled. She said with a steely facial expression, "I feel like a hen who has found that she gave birth to a duck." And the tone of her voice made very clear that she did not consider a duck a good thing to be.

Other discoveries I shared with her and my father that day were equally unwelcome. To my great dismay, my parents understood me to be saying, by reporting my new insights and the changes I was seeing the need for, that I didn't appreciate the many sacrifices they had made for me or the admirable example they had so carefully set. I was saying, they felt, that I saw continuing to follow their pattern as a bad thing to do.

A FIERY TREE

After an afternoon of agonizing conversation with them, I spent a restless night at their house, feeling sick about how I had unintentionally but very seriously hurt them. Then I woke remembering this dream.

> I was entering the front door of a lovely house. Its rooms were arranged like the house I grew up in, but this house was much larger and somehow more elegant. Directly in front of me in its large entry hall was a beautiful tree growing in a large round pot. The tree had three stems of different heights, each topped with healthy green leaves. It obviously had been skillfully pruned, giving it a

striking asymmetrical shape that was perfect for the spot it occupied. Stairs to its right led upward into darkness. A closed door was on the left of the tree. Reaching for its doorknob, my right arm brushed the shortest of the tree's three stems. To my surprise, it snapped in two like a dry, dead stick might do. Even more surprising, the broken top did not fall off. Instead, at the break the stem opened like a hinge, exposing surfaces that were crinkly orange-red, with wisps of smoke rising from them. The wood was obviously burning, and somehow I knew that the whole tree was full of fire inside! Then I woke up.

When I left for home that morning, my mother was furious and all three of us were in tears. I still felt terrible about having hurt my parents. But I also felt that a huge burden I had been carrying needlessly for years had somehow been lifted.

A LIFE-GIVING MESSAGE

For weeks I was so concerned about my parents' pain and anger that I couldn't think about much else. But I couldn't forget the fiery tree. I still can't. Even now, nearly thirty years later, the scene is still as clear and as real to me as any I have ever seen in waking life.

Because of what I had read, when I began to think about my dream I recognized some of what it seemed likely to be saying. I felt that the house represented a new period I was entering. It would resemble the earlier parts of my life but would in some sense be more beautiful and more expansive. The tree seemed to picture my life, and the three stems, my parents and myself. The break was the break I had just made from my lifelong way of relating to my parents. I had learned that in symbolic language circular shapes often portrayed

Jacob woke from his sleep and said, "Surely the Lord is in this place—and I was not aware of it!"
—Genesis 28:16

wholeness, symmetry, and balance. I therefore interpreted the soil-filled circular pot as a way of picturing the wholeness and down-to-earth aspects of life that are the basis for a healthy and well-balanced life. I saw the dark stairs picturing an opportunity to climb to higher levels that I could not yet see, somewhat like the ladder in Jacob's dream described in the Bible (Genesis 28:10-17). The door that I was about to open seemed like a door to a hall closet—the kind of place that typically contains a lot of banished things that need to be looked at and cleaned out.

GOD'S PRESENCE AND POWER

The fire was the main focus of the dream. Fire is dangerous but it is also a valuable source of power and energy. It changes whatever it touches. I remembered that in the Bible God's presence was often portrayed by fire, as in the tongues of flame over the heads of the people present at Pentecost (Acts 2:1-4) and the pillar of fire that led the people of Israel to the Promised Land (Exodus 13:21-22). I also realized that a fiery tree was similar to a burning bush, familiar from the story of Moses in the Bible (Exodus 3:1-15). I therefore felt that my dream was showing me that my life was full of God's presence and power, which I would never have found without making the break from my childish way of functioning. My dream also showed me that I was ready to examine and clean up the baffling things I had stashed away inside my head for so many years, and to climb to new heights that I couldn't yet see.

For a long time that was all I saw, and it seemed like more than enough. But eventually I realized that the fire also pictured anger. I was full of anger, but I hadn't recognized that. All my life I had been taught that anger was not

> *When I was a child, I spoke like a child, I thought like a child, I reasoned like a child. When I became an adult, I put an end to childish ways.*
>
> —1 Corinthians 13:11

permissible—that nice people didn't get angry, and that of course I was a nice person. So I had convinced myself that I was never angry. But from the dream I now realized that I really was seething with anger. I was angry about the church. I was angry about not using my main abilities and pursuing my main interests. The list went on and on.

Now, for the first time, I had started to break from my childlike way of relating to my parents and to every other person and institution whose authority I thought had to be obeyed without question. And that break had enabled me to start recognizing my anger and its causes.

Like fire, anger is both destructive and useful. Smoldering within, it leads to bitterness and meanness, but when the reason for it is identified, it can be a powerful motivation for needed change. Once I saw and acknowledged that I really was angry, I could begin addressing the issues I was angry about.

WAS THERE A LESS PAINFUL WAY?

Looking back on the way in which I dumped all my new insights onto my parents, which caused them so much pain, I wonder if there was a better way for me to make the changes I needed to make. I'm not sure. My new insights had been slowly developing over many years, even before I started realizing it, so when I finally started revealing those insights, they no longer seemed radical to me. I hadn't previously given my parents any inkling of them, however, so my revelation came as a huge shock.

Also, when I was growing up, I almost never heard religious beliefs or political issues discussed. My parents apparently had always agreed between themselves about such subjects, so they had simply presented their views to me as the only right ones, rather than letting me see that others might be worth considering. This lifelong practice contributed to their assuming that as an adult I still accepted all their views as the only right ones, and their being shocked when they suddenly found that was no longer true.

Given these circumstances, should I have waited and made—
or at least revealed—my changes more slowly, in order to soften
the blow for my parents? Maybe so, but I doubt it. I'd already
waited a very long time to really grow up. I'm afraid waiting
longer would have meant never doing it and would have been
detrimental for all three of us in the long run. But I'm not sure.

DOES GOD SPEAK THROUGH DREAMS?

And where was God in my changes? Did my getting new
awareness about myself from my dream show that God speaks
through dreams? Like the answer to many other such questions,
the answer to these depends largely on what we mean by "God."
It may also depend on knowledge about the dreaming process
that hasn't been found yet.

Quite a bit is known now that wasn't known when the Bible
was written—in fact, that wasn't known even a few decades
ago—about the physical processes that happen during dreaming.
Yet much is apparently still unknown about why these processes
happen. But dreaming evidently is somehow part of a process of
restoration that sleep accomplishes. Maybe what dreaming does
for our brain is comparable to what defragmenting the hard drive
does for our computer. Maybe dreaming gets scattered bits and
pieces of information together in our brains in order to use storage
more efficiently and speed up operation. Or maybe dreaming
uses visual images in other ways that promote our emotional or
psychological health. These are only the speculations of some
brain researchers, but if they're anywhere near correct, then
dreaming is evidently a health-giving part of the sleep process.
And dreaming plays its part even when we're not aware of it,
which we usually aren't. The few dreams we remember, sleep
researchers have found, are only a tiny fragment of the countless
dreams that happen constantly while we sleep.

If we see God as a person-like being who loves us and deals
individually with each of us, as many Christians do, then we can

understand our dreams as helpful personal communications from that God. If by "God" we understand instead the all-pervasive system of principles by which the universe and everything in it operates, which is essentially what I now understand "God" to mean, we can see dreaming as a health-promoting natural process. Either way, we can legitimately say that God speaks to us through our dreams as a part of promoting our well-being. And either way, "getting the message," if in fact dreams do in some sense convey messages to us, depends partly on our interpretation. Just as with everything else that people see as messages from God, different people interpret the messages differently, partly because they picture God differently.

LOSING OLD FRIENDS, FINDING NEW ONES

Whatever the source of my new insights may have been, they kept being exhilarating, eye-opening, and in my opinion extremely helpful. And they came in many forms. My reading, especially, kept showing me more changes that might be needed, not only in my personal ways of functioning but also in the church and the wider world. But there was a catch to it all. I didn't know anyone else who read the kinds of things I was reading, or thought about the kinds of things I was thinking about. I wanted someone to discuss it all with and maybe even to work with toward change in the church, but there seemed to be no one. My husband and daughter were supportive, and I had many friends, but they were all busy with other interests. And none of them seemed at all interested in doing the kind of reading and thinking and discussing that now attracted me so strongly.

Soon after I had embarked on my marathon of reading, a group of women church friends and I had started meeting weekly to pray for our church. We hoped to help it emerge more quickly from the damage the recent turmoil had done, and to see how we might personally help that to happen. In addition to praying, we read and discussed books about personal spiritual growth and tried to put what we read into practice. But as I got further into my mysterious personal course of study, that group began changing. New members joined, and the group's original purpose got lost. It became mainly a support group for women in their roles as mothers and wives. Going to lunch together became the group's main focus, and I lost interest. These church friends I had been closest to, who I had thought had concerns similar to mine, no longer seemed to have those concerns. Also, as I moved to a broader understanding of the Bible and the Christian faith, they seemed to move in the opposite direction, to more literalist and doctrine-based views. Now, thirty years later, I still see some of them occasionally, but our main beliefs and interests are now quite different.

As my attachment to those friends loosened, however, a surprising new friend appeared. A new senior pastor came to our church. Like me, he was at midlife, and to my surprise he was thinking about many of the things I was thinking about. And he read books, including books about the very same kinds of things I was reading about! He even thought about what his dreams might mean. I could hardly believe it. I'd never previously heard any pastor mention such things.

Unfortunately, several church members complained continually about this pastor's quoting from books in his sermons. They told him he shouldn't quote from anything but the Bible. That saddened me greatly, because for me he was a godsend. Evidently he was for many others, too, as during his tenure the congregation experienced the greatest numerical growth in its history, and he had the longest tenure of any of its pastors.

REALIZING HOW STARVED I WAS

Besides never having had a pastor who mentioned reading serious books, I had also never before had a pastor who asked me what I was interested in or what I did when I wasn't doing the typical women's church volunteer jobs. But this pastor did.

Shortly before he arrived, my father-in-law had had a stroke that left him unable to function. I had been heavily involved in community volunteer projects, but when his stroke happened I had just finished a big one, a term as president of the local arts center, and no other one was in sight. Also, my daughter was now in high school and driving and no longer needed all of the daily mothering duties that had filled much of my time earlier. I suddenly had time to spare, so I was doing much of the necessary hospital sitting with my father-in-law.

Still following my mysterious personal custom-designed course of study, I used a lot of that hospital-sitting time for reading. I mentally conversed with the authors as I read, by underlining and making marginal notes in the books and by journaling. When the new pastor came to the hospital to visit my father-in-law, a long-time member of our congregation, he often found me reading and writing, and we talked about our mutual interests.

Doing all this reading and then finding this kindred spirit made me even more aware of how starved I had become, not only for others who shared my interests but also for the intellectual activity I had mostly been without for the twenty years since I quit my job to get married.

AN EMPTY FEELING

It hadn't previously occurred to me that neither the duties of being a mother nor my involvement in typical volunteer jobs would last for my whole life. Now, however, I had finished all of life that I had foreseen. I saw nothing interesting to look forward to. That empty feeling, together with my starvation for mental activity and kindred spirits, finally made me feel desperate enough to get out and look for the other people I felt must be "out there" somewhere. I knew there must be other people interested in reading, thinking, and maybe even doing something about the things I had become so interested in. I became determined to find them.

To find the mental activity, I started looking for a college course to take, but no nearby university offered the interdisciplinary combination of subjects I wanted—religion, theology, depth psychology, religious experience, and other related topics. Finally to my great surprise I discovered that the schools that offered this mixture were seminaries. I'd never remotely considered attending a seminary, but now I was feeling desperate enough to consider it. To my even greater surprise, the closest seminary that had a curriculum broad enough to serve my purpose was the one I was most familiar with, my denomination's seminary at the university I had graduated from almost twenty-five years earlier. I'd known of that seminary for years, but I hadn't had a good opinion of it. My family and fellow church members had always said it was dangerously liberal. Still, when I looked at its catalog, I saw it was what I was looking for. I daringly signed up for one course.

I chose that course partly because it met at 1:00, only once a week. That schedule gave me time to prepare breakfast and make the beds before leaving home. And after class, I could get home in time to prepare dinner and go to choir rehearsal or whatever other activity was scheduled for the evening. I wouldn't fail to do any of my duties, and I wouldn't disrupt anyone else's life.

Getting to the seminary required a two-and-a-half-hour drive, and my parents had always warned me about the dangers of a woman driving alone on the highway, but now I did it anyway.

I KNEW I WAS IN THE RIGHT PLACE

During my first course, few of my friends at home knew what I was doing, because I kept quiet about it, not wanting to be seen as odd. But soon they noticed and began asking questions. At a social event, a friend would say casually, "What have you been doing lately? I've missed seeing you."

I'd start with the least revealing answer I could come up with, hoping I wouldn't have to say more. "I'm taking a college course."

Then the friend would guess a nearby college and I'd say no, hoping she wouldn't ask anything else.

But admitting where I was going brought more questions. "You're driving that far? What are you taking that you couldn't get somewhere closer?" Then it got sticky.

"I'm taking a course at Perkins."

That brought a wide-eyed look, and then, "You're not going to be a *preacher*, are you?"

"No, I just wanted to learn more about some things that interest me."

Then came the inevitable follow-up question, "What course are you taking?"

"I'm taking 'Interpretation of Dreams.'" At that point the conversation always ended quickly, with the friend leaving to find a saner and safer person to talk to.

I soon got past my reluctance, however, and started bravely admitting the strange thing I was doing, without caring what anyone would think about it. Also, I found that the seminary had a master's degree program that could include almost anything I wanted from the curriculum. I kept going for three years and came out with a degree.

During those years I discovered tape-recorded books and loved listening as I drove. I loved seeing sunrises when I left home at 5:00 A.M. to get to 8:00 classes in some semesters. But above all, I loved what I found in every class. As soon as I went to my first class, I knew I was in the right place.

ANOTHER LIFE-CHANGING PROGRAM

Soon after starting my first seminary course, I found my way into another surprising and life-changing experience. In a church newspaper I read that my denomination was starting a new program called The Academy for Spiritual Formation.[8] It would

---

[8]www.upperroom.org/academy/.

meet in Nashville for five days every three months for two years.
A pilot group of laity and clergy from all over the United States
was being enlisted for it. The newspaper article listed some of the
faculty and the books that would be used as texts. I could hardly
believe my eyes. Several of the faculty members were authors of
books I'd been reading, and several of the texts were books I'd
been wanting to discuss—another surprising godsend.

Being in the Academy was exhilarating, and not only because
of the presenters and the reading and the kindred spirits I found
there. It also gave me the opportunity to get out into the wider
world and feel like an individual in my own right, after years of
feeling I was only a wife and mother and doer of background
jobs. To get to Academy sessions, I flew alone for the first time in
twenty-five years. I talked to people I sat by on the planes, since my
outgoing husband wasn't there to do the talking as he usually did
when we flew together. When I was in airports, no one pointed
out the restrooms to me as he usually did. When I crossed streets,
no one told me the light had turned green and it was time to
walk, another habit of his, undoubtedly well intentioned but not
conducive to my feeling like a competent adult. When I occasionally
went with Academy women friends to nearby restaurants after
evening sessions, we didn't talk about husbands or children, the
main conversational topics of my women friends at home. And
when I took part in Academy discussions, people acted as if what
I said was worth hearing. As a new friend of those years said about
such experiences, when like me she was attending seminary as a lay
woman at midlife, "It's like being a real person, isn't it!"

These experiences began showing me that even though some
of my thinking made me a misfit in my family and my home
church and community, and made me feel alone, there were other
settings in which I was far from alone. But coming back home
was always a jolt. My flights home from Academy sessions and
my drives home from seminary classes always seemed like the
decompression chambers in which deep-sea divers have to stay

temporarily before returning to the surface after having spent time in the depths.

Then, when my time in seminary and the Academy ended and I was back in my home town and my local church for good, the contrast to what I'd been experiencing at seminary and the Academy made me feel more alone and more like a misfit than ever. But these experiences had also confirmed my feeling that churches needed to make some changes if they were to keep people from feeling unwelcome merely because their views differed from the majority. That confirmation convinced me that I needed to stop keeping quiet.

ENDING YEARS OF SILENCE

An old joke tells about a boy who for his first ten years never said a word. Doctors tested him and found nothing that made him unable to speak, but still he didn't speak. Then suddenly at the dinner table one night when he was ten, he said, "The soup's cold!" His parents were baffled. They asked him, "If you were able to speak, why didn't you say anything before now?"

"It's simple," he said. "Everything has been okay until now."

That's essentially the story of my experience in the church. For nearly fifty years I rarely spoke up about anything, but when I became convinced that change was needed, I started speaking. My keeping quiet wasn't because I had thought everything was okay, however. It was because when I saw things I suspected weren't okay, I assumed the problem was only with me. I assumed that everything in the church actually made sense but that, unlike everyone else, I hadn't yet seen how. I had kept relying on my mother's explanation—when you get older you will see why the existing way is the right way, or the best way, or the necessary way. If you wait long enough, it will all become clear. You'll eventually catch on. You'll see that if you disagree, you're the one who's wrong.

WHAT WAS WRONG WASN'T JUST WITH ME

But finally, through the surprising changes I was experiencing at midlife—reading and thinking about new subjects, talking with newly discovered kindred spirits, and learning more about myself and other people—I started seeing that what was wrong wasn't entirely with me. I needed to make some changes in my ways of functioning, but also there really were things that needed changing in the church and the world, if we wanted to follow the teaching and example of Jesus. And other people "out there" were noticing some of those things just as I was.

As I began getting involved in church-related activities and groups beyond my local congregation, I starting finding some of those people. I found that most of them felt just as alone in their home churches as I felt in mine. Especially, I found many who were dismayed by the sexism they recognized in the church and the wider world. I got to know other women who, like me, had been given the impression that their interests, opinions, and abilities didn't matter, and that God wanted them to keep quiet and stay in the background in the church and elsewhere. I met many who were concerned about the harm being done by the all-masculine language that was used constantly in worship services. I discovered clergywomen and female seminary professors who were getting lower salaries than men in the same jobs, or who were being treated merely as men's helpers. All of us had become convinced that these problems were important and that change was needed, but in our home churches and among our friends at home, we knew almost no one who recognized the need for change.

A LETTER TO KEEP KINDRED SPIRITS ENCOURAGED

As I became more and more convinced of the need for change and discovered more and more of these concerned women and a few similarly concerned men, I started thinking about writing a letter every now and then to keep all of us reminded that we weren't alone and that our concerns were important. My idea was to send this letter to the kindred spirits I'd met at the events I'd been attending. I assumed I could come up with a mailing list of one or two hundred names, which seemed like a lot. But when I got really serious about sending such a letter, I kept losing my nerve. I'd never heard of anyone doing such a thing, and my stay-in-the-background-and-keep-quiet pattern kept telling me it would be ridiculous and pointless.

Still, I couldn't shake the idea. Finally I decided to act on it even if it was crazy. The more I thought about it, though, the more I saw the need to go beyond my original idea. Writing only about the so-called women's issues and writing only to people who were already convinced of their importance wouldn't promote the needed changes. I realized that change wasn't likely to happen in the church until a lot more members saw the need for it.

I realized, too, that awareness about other church-related issues was needed. Lay people needed a greater role in decision-making. Churches needed to stop using outdated language and clinging to outdated beliefs. Members needed to be given the kinds of information I'd become aware of through my reading and seminary classes. If I was going to spend the time, effort, and money necessary for sending the letter I was considering, I needed to write about a much broader range of topics than I had originally intended, and to use a much broader and larger mailing list.

I HAD WHAT WAS NECESSARY

I had a computer and had become experienced at using it. Its software included newsletter layouts and clip art, plus provisions for a database of names and addresses. I was able to pay for printing and postage. I now had a seminary education and the Academy experience, added to years of reading and thinking about the kind of topics I wanted to write about, and the interest necessary for learning more. Also, I was neither a church employee nor a clergyman's wife or daughter, so I would risk no status or income by saying things that differed from the church's party line.

I also felt I might be a useful bridge between laity and clergy. At seminary I had learned to speak the language of clergy and academics. I had gotten to know clergy who spoke with me about concerns they didn't often reveal to lay church members or even fellow clergy. Yet from my decades as a volunteer in the church and community, I was used to speaking lay language and seeing practical viewpoints that clergy and academics often seemed to miss.

The more I thought about it, the more I realized that I had all the necessary resources for sending the kind of letter I now had in mind. I started experimenting with writing it.

Several possible names came to mind. A friend suggested "Connections," and that seemed better than anything I'd thought of, so I adopted it without much thought. I decided to use yellow paper to make the letter stand out among recipients' mail. (A few years later a marketing-professor friend whom I asked for advice told me yellow was unwise because of the connotation of "yellow journalism," but by then it seemed too late to change.)

For a mailing list, to the names of kindred spirits I'd originally had in mind, I added other people from various groups I'd been part of. Then I added some local and regional church leaders whose views I didn't know. At the last minute I added my denomination's United States bishops. The final list contained about twelve hundred names, which seemed huge to me. But by that time, I was feeling really daring. I felt I had nothing to lose by doing this unheard-of thing, so I might as well risk it. In November 1992 I mailed the first issue of *Connections*, feeling as if I were sending it into a black hole with no idea what might happen to it.

THE LIST MUSHROOMED

To my amazement, I started hearing from recipients immediately, and none of them said, "You must be crazy!" Instead, they said, "I'm so glad someone is speaking up about these things!" Many asked, "How can I get you to add some names to your mailing list?" Most surprising, several sent checks to help with printing and postage, though I hadn't asked for money—hadn't even imagined that anyone would be willing to pay for what I wanted to write. My list mushroomed, the responses kept coming, and almost all were appreciative.

Over the years, in addition to the many people who've asked to be added to my list I've also added names of people who have special opportunity to influence the church, especially delegates to my denomination's official decision-making bodies. My mailing list has now grown to include several thousand people. It includes members of at least twelve church denominations and some non-churchgoers. They're laity and clergy in every United States state and a few other countries. I send *Connections* by e-mail now (my preferred way, and the only way I can send it outside the United States) as well as by mailing paper copies. Many recipients tell me they forward every issue to a list of their own. Many now get *Connections* each month from my website, *www.connectionsonline. org*, and several groups and individuals have links to it on their sites or blogs. Thus I have no idea how many people now get *Connections* each month.

The longer I write *Connections*, the more convinced I become that there are many people who feel like misfits in relation to the church but who are reluctant to speak because they think they're alone. One of my main reasons for continuing to write *Connections* is to make more of these thinking people aware that they're actually not alone, that many of their observations are undoubtedly correct, that their views are important for the church to hear, and that they therefore need to be making their voices heard.

LED OUT OF THE PRISON TO SPEAK

Reading the Bible in recent years, I've come to see the temple of ancient Israel as analogous to the institutional church of our time.

Several scriptures about the temple seem especially applicable to our dealings with today's institutional church. They include powerful images like this one: "During the night an angel of the Lord opened the prison doors, brought them out, and said, 'Go, stand in the temple and tell the people the whole message about this life'" (Acts 5:19-20).

The new insights and information that came unexpectedly to me while I was still in the dark prison of my former ways of thinking and functioning were like an angel that opened the doors and led me out. Now I feel I need to stand in the temple and speak, and that's what I'm trying to do. I'm trying to encourage the many other people who feel like misfits but see things that need the church's attention, to stand in *their* temples and speak also.

I believe that thinking, perceptive church members urgently need to be speaking in the church, saying what they understand to be the whole Christian message. We need to help other members see beyond the abridged, distorted version of the message that is so often all they hear. We also need to let the world hear the whole message.

NOT JUST "A NICE NUT"

Unfortunately, speaking like this doesn't always bring appreciation. I get appreciation and support continually from the wider church, but very little from my local congregation. Ironically, from that group in which I've been so active in so many ways for nearly fifty years, I've gotten mainly rejection in recent years, and that hurts.

For years I've been well aware that many congregation members disagreed with some of my views. When I've spoken up in choir rehearsals to ask that we sing "us" or "all" instead of "men," or "God" instead of "he," the main reaction has been cold silence, rolling eyes, and snickers. Also, for several years I haven't been asked to lead any class or discussion, and I'm no longer in any church decision-making bodies.

Until recently, however, I naively assumed that most members merely saw me in the way a misfit friend recently told me her congregation saw her, as "a nice nut." I didn't realize that so many felt that our differences meant I should have no voice in the church. I certainly never imagined that they would shun me and take active steps to silence me. But now that has happened.

Such treatment is minor, of course, compared to the mistreatment that countless other Christians have experienced over the centuries, when they've expressed views that differed from the majority or threatened the power of religious or political leaders. Still, it's shocking and painful when church members attack, stifle, shun, or oust fellow Christians who disagree with them. Wouldn't it be kinder and more productive to discuss issues openly, to look for more information about them, and to recognize that Christians can legitimately come to different conclusions about how Christian principles may apply to them?

III

Many Misfits with the Same Messages

WHAT IS MOST STRIKING to me about the responses to *Connections* I get is that the same themes keep appearing in so many of them. This pattern should be telling us something. When concerns are so widespread, our churches need to be aware of them. We need to recognize them as evidence of changes we need to make. The following messages that I get over and over, from current and former churchgoers, are saying things the church needs to heed.

- **A painful step and a hard decision**

  The Christians I hear from who have dropped out or chosen to attend church less often after having been active in it have not made this change hastily or impulsively—far from it. Indeed, many of them have seriously examined their own beliefs, the Bible's origin and contents, the history of Christianity and its doctrines, and the views of a variety of writers and speakers. One of these Christians who has left the church says, "It has been a slow process for me to arrive at my present place. My gradual 'drop-away' from the church has taken at least twenty or more years." Among the *Connections* readers I hear from, that's more the rule than the exception.

- **Stronger faith without attending church**

  David Dykes, who presents public seminars featuring leading biblical scholars, tells me he hears this paradox repeatedly from attenders. "At every one of our events," he reports, "people tell me that hearing what they've heard here about what early Christianity was like and how the Bible developed has changed their lives. And they ask why, when they're very active in a church, they've never heard it before." That speaks volumes. Why aren't church leaders paying more attention to the damage being done not only by some of what people are hearing in their churches but also by what they're failing to hear?

- **Surprised by not missing worship**

  Many readers say they don't miss it when they stop attending, even after many years of attending regularly and participating actively in the church in other ways. "For too long I have sat in church and been bored to tears," one reader wrote. "I went because, well, because it is Sunday and you go to church." Many of us misfits have felt like that, even if the feeling hasn't made us drop out. The fact that people who stop going to our worship don't miss it says a lot that we need to hear and pay attention to.

- **Being fed isn't necessary**

  The Christians I hear from would like to be fed by worship services, but they could be satisfied with something more modest. They just want the services not to hinder them. One wrote, "I just want a worship setting that doesn't get in the way of my experience of God." They don't want what happens in worship services to keep them from being aware of God's presence.

- **Concerns that aren't superficial**

  Most of these Christians aren't hung up on styles of worship. Most of them can live with video screens on sanctuary walls, or a loaf instead of a wafer at communion, or singers wearing street clothes instead of choir robes. They don't have anything against guitars or dancers in the sanctuary, or modern songs instead of anthems by Bach and Handel. They're concerned instead about what is being communicated by *whatever* style of worship services they attend.

- **Very little is being communicated**

  Many misfits mention that in the services they attend, hardly anything is being said, especially in the songs and prayers. They are left cold by popular contemporary praise songs and scripture songs—the kind some people call "cotton-candy songs," that vanish before you can sink your teeth into them, or "7–11 songs," that seem to have only seven words repeated eleven times. These misfits don't want to be a captive audience, either, for the mindless "weejus" prayers in which sentence after sentence starts with "Lord, we just . . ."

- **What we hear doesn't match**

  What we hear in church doesn't seem to jibe with what we've learned from other sources. What we hear the church saying about the world, the nature of God, human beings, the Bible and its relation to other religions' sacred writings, or the nature of religion in general rarely matches the best current thinking about these subjects.

- **Focusing on the past**

  Today's Christians communicate by the latest methods—cell phones, laptops, blogs, Facebook, I-Phones and Blackberries and MP3's—so why do their portrayals of Christianity so often focus on the past? And yet they rarely look to pertinent parts of the past. Learning about the time of Jesus or Paul could help us interpret what the Bible says, but we don't often do that. Much of what happens in church looks back instead to only a few centuries ago, by using the language of the King James Version of the Bible or continuing to follow all the practices of our denomination's founders. And many churchgoers cling to traditions such as American gospel hymns and 1950s-style "revivals" that are actually only a few decades old, defending them as if they had been started by Jesus. Is this mainly due to nostalgia?

- **A long-outdated picture of the universe**

  In prayers, songs, and rituals, we misfits long for an image of God that fits today's understanding of the natural world or at least acknowledges other images as metaphorical. Instead, in church we hear about a God who looks down on a flat earth from the sky, capriciously helping some people but punishing others with cancers, fatal auto wrecks, or tidal waves. One *Connections* reader wrote, "I cringe when the prayers are offered." Another wrote that when he goes to church and hears a description of God that seems to contradict everything he knows, "it's as if the church is insulting God with its worship— or if that's too harsh, at least selling God short."

- **An urgent need for community**

  A brief time of "passing the peace" or holding hands during worship services doesn't serve the purpose. In fact, these practices are turn-offs for many. My readers often write about feeling desperate—*desperate!*—for kindred spirits with whom they can talk seriously and openly about religious beliefs, current issues, and their own lives. To find safe places for this kind of conversation, however, many say they've had to look outside the church. One said that finding like-minded people to talk with was like an underground or "closet Christian" experience. That's ironic, because Christianity is about relating not only to God but also to the people and the world around us. If we have to hide in any kind of closet in order to talk about our real concerns and find true community, something's seriously wrong in our churches.

Here's how the lack of community looks to one person who told me she'd finally stopped attending after years of regular involvement in her church. "I really miss having a loving community, but that wasn't one anyway. When I raised questions or mentioned the possible need for change, people resented me as though I had invented the idea or was the only one trying to change." Another reader explained that what was important to him was being among people who weren't locked down by tradition and who had a passion for truth, in a setting where that passion was allowed to emerge.

Because they so rarely hear anyone else expressing feelings or views like these, many Christians who share them have thought they were entirely alone, so they haven't understood the reason for their feelings. Often, they have simply assumed there was something wrong with them. They haven't spoken up about their concerns, because they thought that if they revealed their real views or questions, they'd be seen as sinful, ignorant, or even stupid.

In this kind of atmosphere, even a distant, faint message of hope is better than none. One *Connections* reader wrote recently, echoing many others, "Thank you for your efforts to reach and validate those of us who feel so lonely in our beliefs."

The people who write me about feeling like misfits aren't lukewarm, irresponsible, uninterested, uncommitted, or unchristian. On the contrary, they think seriously about their beliefs and care deeply about the church. That is, they care about the purposes they believe the church is meant to pursue, based on what they understand Jesus to have taught and demonstrated. They see the need to take the Christian faith more seriously, not less. They want to be more committed to following Jesus, not less.

Reactions like those I'm reporting here strike a chord not only with adult lay church members, but also with many teenagers, clergy, and academics. "You have put your hands on one of the crucial issues in the life of the church," theologian Joerg Rieger wrote me. "How frustrating it is to deal with a church that does not expect any challenges or surprises from God and that acts as if we know all there is to know about God. I know many people who share your feelings, seminary faculty included. My school-age children could not agree with you more."

Rieger's work often takes him to places as far away as Argentina, South Africa, and Germany, as well as to many parts of the United States, lecturing and meeting with clergy and laypeople. "Even in other countries," he reports, "people have similar feelings. Some have been active in church for decades but no longer know how to relate to it." Like many other concerned Christians, he sees such alienation less as an individual failing than as a failure on the part of the church. "There is no lack of faith in God," he finds. "Faith in God is the reason for questioning the church. We have something of a movement here, of faithful people who can't stand church any more. This does not seem to be about demanding small changes here or there. It seems to be about fundamental issues."

If that's true, it may be a hopeful sign. Yet what must we do as a church, to address those issues and make the needed changes happen?

STRUGGLING CHURCHES IN A SUFFERING WORLD

We hear a lot today about thriving megachurches, but there are also plenty of struggling churches. Many older and smaller churches suffer from not having enough members to keep their buildings maintained and salaries paid. Urban churches fight to maintain a vital presence in the inner city. Many such churches desperately want to know how to reach more people, how to make a greater difference in their communities. At the same time, many misfits are desperately looking for a church that will take them seriously. Focusing on these misfits could help churches reach people they're now turning off.

United Church of Christ pastor Eric Elnes calls these turned-off people the "spiritually homeless." Whether they've been ousted from a church, have chosen to leave, or are still hanging on, they feel alienated from the faith community. Many identify themselves as Christians, yet don't actively participate in any church.

Elnes co-founded an organization called CrossWalk America to host a walk from Phoenix to Washington, D.C. in 2006. He and his companions fostered conversations along the way. They asked people what it means in today's world, in a period of growing fundamentalism in our nation, to be progressive Christians who think seriously about the Bible's message of loving God, neighbor, and self.

Elnes reports that the walkers found thousands of spiritually homeless people on their journey. They found them in small towns and rural areas as well as in large cities, and among a variety of racial and ethnic groups.[9] That means most churches are surrounded by people who are spiritually homeless. But to provide the faith communities that these misfits long for, churches would have to look honestly at why they're not attracting them now.

A SHOCKING CONTRAST TO PAUL'S PICTURE

Many of us misfits are still hanging on in the church even though we're dismayed by much that we see happening in it. We still feel that the church has something to offer that the world needs. We're still at least a tiny bit hopeful about being able to help more people see how following the teaching of Jesus could make life better for people. So a lot of us are still participating in our churches, even if only in minimal ways.

Other misfits, however, including a lot that I hear from, have become part of what retired Episcopal Bishop John Shelby Spong calls "the church alumni association." These Christians were active in churches earlier in their lives, but they became too turned off by the church to be willing to keep participating. Some no longer even consider themselves to be Christians.

---

[9]Eric Elnes, *Asphalt Jesus: Finding a New Faith Along the Highways of America* (San Francisco: Wiley/Jossey-Bass, 2007).

For some of these church alumni/ae, however, leaving wasn't totally their own choice. They're a group some pastors call "the dechurched," in contrast to the people church leaders call "the unchurched," who have never been part of any church. The dechurched have been ordered to leave a congregation or at least have been made to feel so unwelcome that they finally left.

Another label I've heard used for these ousted members is "dismembered." That's a shocking contrast to the apostle Paul's comparison of the church to a human body whose members are all valuable. When a body is dismembered, it can no longer function or it is at least severely impaired. When any of its members are cut off, its life blood spills out and is lost. That's a dreadful condition for a church to be in. Yet by ousting members who differ from the majority, some churches are deliberately dismembering themselves.

CHURCHES REFUSING TO PLACATE
WHINY CHRISTIANS

According to a 2006 *Wall Street Journal* article, well-known Christian pastor and author Rick Warren teaches pastors how to get rid of these unwanted members, in connection with teaching the pastors how to attract new members. Warren's congregation and its nonprofit arm have trained several hundred thousand pastors worldwide, says the *Journal* article, and part of the training teaches them how to deal with opposition to the changes that Warren's methods will require in their churches. There the methods get mean. The *Journal* article reports a trainer telling pastors to "speak to critical members, then help them leave if they don't stop objecting." And that's not all. If the members join a different church after leaving, "pastors should call their new minister and suggest that [they] be barred from any leadership roles."

"There are moments when you've got to play hardball," this article quotes another trainer as saying. "You cannot transition a church . . . and placate every whiny Christian along the way."[10]

---

[10]Susan Sataline, "A Popular Strategy for Church Growth Splits Congregants Across the United States," *The Wall Street Journal*, Sept. 5, 2006.

A few months later another *Journal* article opened with the glaring headline "Banned from church" and a caricature of God's finger pointing a church member toward the exit. "Reviving an ancient practice," the article reported, "churches are exposing sinners and shunning those who won't repent." In a growing movement, according to the article, many churches are ousting or shunning members not just for sins such as theft and adultery but also for merely skipping services or criticizing church leaders. And the groups this article mentioned as shunning or banning members weren't just predictably narrow fundamentalist sects. Some were mainline congregations.[11]

When a secular, business-oriented newspaper with international circulation reports church developments like these, it looks like evidence that church misfits are becoming not only more numerous but also more widely recognized as significant for the world, not just for the church.

CONSTANT MOVEMENT IN UNITED STATES RELIGION

The 2008 United States Religious Landscape Survey by The Pew Forum on Religion and Public Life gives a picture that's much broader than what comes from anecdotal reports like the ones I happened to read in *The Wall Street Journal* and the ones I get from *Connections* readers. However, the Pew survey's picture is similar. It shows a large number of people becoming disenchanted and leaving the religions they've been part of. The Pew survey found that more than a fourth of United States adults have left the faith in which they were raised, to change to another religion or no religion. Within Protestantism, this survey showed, about 44% of adults have changed their religious affiliation. They have moved from one Protestant denomination to another, joined one after not having been affiliated with any religion, or dropped out.[12]

---

[11] Alexandra Alter, "Banned from church." *The Wall Street Journal*, Jan. 18, 2008, W1.
[12] http://religions.pewforum.org/.

In a way, articles and surveys like these seem encouraging. They seem to say that more Christians are thinking about their beliefs and paying attention to whether their churches are doing anything that really matters. These reports may say that fewer Christians are willing to keep attending uninspiring worship services or to keep accepting unconvincing doctrines and following autocratic leaders.

Articles like those in the *Journal*, however, also remind us that a lot of churches are becoming less willing to put up with diverse views among their members, and that's discouraging.

AN URGENT NEED FOR DIVERSITY

My experiences in the church, plus what I hear so often from other church misfits, have convinced me that many of our congregations and our denominations' decision-making bodies need a lot more diversity of views than they now include. Having more diverse views within our churches could help not only the churches but also the world.

Many mainline denominations have realized that they need more diversity of some kinds. In the United States, mainline denominations are becoming increasingly aware that their membership is older than the population. They're realizing, therefore, that they need to reach younger people with the Christian message and make them feel welcome in the church. Many denominations also realize they need greater racial and ethnic diversity. They realize, too, that their physical facilities and activities need to be accessible to people with diverse levels of physical ability. Churches haven't yet made the needed amount of progress toward these kinds of diversity, but many are now at least making efforts toward needed change.

The need to encourage diverse views in the church is a different story, however. Many church members are apparently so sure that their interpretation of Christianity and the Bible is the only right one and that their picture of God is complete and totally correct, that they are actively trying to stifle or even oust the people whose views differ from theirs. I was surprised to learn that when Eric Elnes and his CrossWalk America group made their walk across the United States, the greatest antagonism they encountered didn't come from their saying that homosexuality wasn't sinful. Rather, the strongest opposition came from their saying that Christianity was not the only route to God or the only religion with the truth. Even when Christians accept other kinds of diversity, many won't admit that diverse beliefs about God or diverse interpretations of the Bible's contents should be allowed in the church.

WHY ALLOW DIVERSITY?
WHY BOTHER WITH THE MISFITS?

Why should diverse beliefs or interpretations be allowed? Isn't everyone in the church supposed to be Christian? And doesn't that require that all believe certain things? Why should the church pay any attention to the people whose views differ from the majority? Why not just keep ignoring them or trying to get rid of them?

Above all, it's because if we really believe the world needs more of the kind of love and justice that Jesus advocated, as Christians claim to believe, we can't afford to reject the help of anyone who wants to help promote those qualities. We can't afford to shun people who want to join us in working to decrease poverty or protect the environment, just because their image of God or their interpretation of a certain Bible passage is different from ours. To make a dent in these huge problems, we need all the help we can get. We need more help than just what we can get from the people whose opinions are exactly the same as our own.

Another reason for actively seeking diversity in the church is that hearing a variety of views and getting information from various sources helps us clarify our beliefs and opinions. We all need some kindred spirits to support us, but if we listen only to the people whose experience has been like ours, whose understanding of the Bible's meaning is like ours, and who know no more about the Bible than we do, we get a view of Christianity that's not very reliable. Also, we're likely to know only about the way it is practiced within a very limited area. We can easily confuse our personal preferences and cultural customs with the essentials of the Christian message. And we can get the badly mistaken impression that we're right about everything.

There's another important reason, too, for welcoming our churches' misfits and taking seriously what they're saying. Throughout the Bible and later history, the people Christians claim to admire most—the people who have turned out to be expressing what most Christians see as God's will—have been misfits. Few have been the official leaders or even docile members of the religious "establishment" of their time. In fact, many have actively opposed its leaders and the views of the majority of its members. They have worked to make changes in that religious establishment, sometimes at the cost of their lives. They haven't been unquestioning supporters of their governments, either, or followers of all the customs their society considered essential. Some have protested against their government and even broken laws. Many have openly violated social customs. As a result, we now call these brave people heroes or even saints.

OUR MAIN SPIRITUAL HEROES WERE MISFITS

Jesus opposed both the religious establishment and the government of his day. In efforts to promote church attendance, today's church leaders sometimes cite scriptures that mention his regular attendance at the synagogue, but according to the gospels he often broke its rules and spoke against its traditions. Some of today's leaders also cite scriptures that seem to advocate support of all governments, yet Jesus's open opposition to the Roman Empire cost him his life. He continually emphasized how different the kingdom of God was from the religious and secular systems of his day. He regularly associated with social outcasts, too. Jesus was a misfit.

So were countless others of our spiritual heroes. The prophets we read about in the Old Testament. The early Christian martyrs. The founders of Protestant denominations. Martin Luther King, Jr., Gandhi, Susan B. Anthony, and numerous other prominent opponents of injustice in more recent years.

WE WOULDN'T WANT JESUS OR JEREMIAH IN OUR CHURCH

What's ironic about our attitude toward these spiritual heroes is that we claim to admire them but we wouldn't want people like them in our churches. They'd be too disruptive. They'd cause uncomfortable conflict. They wouldn't follow the rules. Some of their behavior would embarrass us and our friends. They wouldn't be fun to be with. They'd be constantly criticizing us. They'd be criticizing our church and our governments, too. They'd be misfits.

The world notices this attitude and often tunes us out because of it. People outside the church see us talking a good game but not playing it, when as Christians we claim to admire compassion and justice and nonviolence but don't want our friends, churches, or governments to practice them. If we want the world to take the church seriously, we need to welcome the misfits who practice the qualities we claim to admire. That means we need to welcome diverse views.

Diana Butler Bass, a scholar who studies American Protestantism, wisely points out how important diversity is for churches. She has studied fifty thriving mainline Protestant congregations across the United States, to see what enables them to thrive. She found that it is innovative use of traditional Christian practices, and diversity is one she found to be especially important. Bass has consistently seen how the lack of diversity keeps churches from thriving, besides hurting individuals. "When Christians elevate uniformity," she has found, "shunning, excommunication, heresy trials, inquisitions, schism, crusades, and religious warfare are among the predictable results." Her study of the history of religion shows her that "the Christian West has been marked by a twisted insistence on sameness—especially in belief—that has led to a sadly ironic result: vast numbers of people who doubt or reject Christianity on the basis of its hypocrisy." She asks, "How can a religion that speaks so eloquently of love so brutally destroy its questioners, its dissenters, its innovators, and its competitors?"[13] Good question.

JESUS WARNED US ABOUT THIS

Jesus apparently warned his followers about trying to get rid of people they saw as misfits. The gospels show him illustrating this with a story about the need to let weeds remain among the wheat. He warned that we could be wrong about which plants were weeds and which were wheat, and pull up the wrong ones by mistake (Matthew 13:27-30). We read also about his telling people their assumptions were mistaken, about who was in the Kingdom of God and who wasn't (Matthew 21:31). We find him telling his disciples not to try to stop people whose methods differed from his (Mark 9:40). We often see him reminding people that many of God's standards of measuring what's right and what's wrong are different from human standards. We also find him talking about having other sheep in other folds (John 10:16).

If we really admire the spiritual heroes we say we admire, therefore, and if we want to follow Jesus, we need to pay attention to some of the misfits who are in our churches or have been ousted from them. We need to pay attention to some who have never been in any church, too. Some of them are seeing and saying things that the church needs to hear and heed.

THE BEST THINGS HAVE HAPPENED ON THE EDGE

Episcopal priest Barbara Brown Taylor reminds us that history's misfits have included Martin Luther, Joan of Arc, Francis of

---

[13]Diana Butler Bass, *Christianity for the Rest of Us: How the Neighborhood Church Is Transforming the Faith* (New York: HarperSanFrancisco, 2006), 150.

Assisi, and Copernicus, as well as Jesus. "All these people," Taylor observes, "made unauthorized choices in their love of God. They saw things they were not supposed to see or said things they were not supposed to say. They wondered about things they were not supposed to wonder about, and when Mother Church told them to stop they did not obey her. Some of them died for their disobedience while others were locked in their rooms. Still others were sent out of the house and told to never come back." However, "many of them are spiritual heroes now. At least one of them is revered as the Son of God."

"Given their amazing comebacks," Taylor asks us, "might it be time for people of good faith to allow that God's map is vast, with room on it for both a center and an edge?" Here's what she feels we especially need to keep in mind in answering that question. "While the center may be the place where the stories of the faith are preserved, the edge is the place where the best of them happened."[14]

UNSETTLING GIFTS FROM GOD

I'm afraid we too often stifle the "edge people" in our churches. The anger some of them express is likely to make us want to avoid or even stifle them, but doing that is not wise. "However unsettling righteously angry people may be, their capacity to feel anger toward and to seek redress of wrongs in the world is one of God's greatest gifts to them and to us as well," points out emeritus seminary professor Leroy Howe. "Rather than our criticism and our judgment, they need and deserve our appreciation and support."

"We can render this appreciation and support most especially," Howe suggests, "by (1) honoring their gift of discernment and the anger that inevitably must accompany it, (2) listening closely enough to create opportunities for them to assess their anger

---

[14]Barbara Brown Taylor, *Leaving Church: A Memoir of Faith*. (New York: HarperSan-Francisco, 2006), 177.

objectively, (3) guiding them toward more effective ways of expressing their anger constructively, and (4) encouraging them when their energy is at a low ebb." In addition, Leroy Howe emphasizes, "Accompanying any and all of these expressions should be constant prayer with and for them that their feelings and actions will bear fruit." After all, he reminds us, "it is a good thing to feel angry about injustice of every kind. God intends for us to feel angry about such things and for our anger to give us the energy we need to change them for the better. . . . The affirmation [that these angry people need] begins by honoring the anger that societal evils inspire in them, especially when others begin to tell them in not-so-subtle ways that getting along by going along is the more acceptable course."[15]

It's important to remember, finds Howe, that ". . . righteous anger is more than a way merely to fulminate against evil; it is a resource for resisting and transforming it."[16] It's one of the resources that misfits can contribute to the church, so we make a serious mistake when we keep that resource hidden rather than take advantage of it.

THE MINISTRY OF IRRITATION

Benedictine sister Joan Chittister makes a related point. She finds that by speaking up, misfits perform a needed "ministry of irritation." It works like the sand that irritates the oyster but causes a pearl to form. She urges us to remember that throughout history ordinary people who have simply seen the truth and said it have been God's instruments for changing the world.[17] Are any misfits in your church furnishing a "ministry of irritation" whose pearls you're not allowing to form?

---

[15]Leroy Howe, *Angry People in the Pews: Managing Anger in the Church* (Valley Forge, PA: Judson Press, 2001), 98–99.

[16]Howe, 103.

[17]Joan Chittister, "Mysticism, Empowerment, and Resistance" seminar presented by the D.L. Dykes, Jr. Foundation in Austin, Texas, May 18–20, 2006.

Chittister reminds us that "people currently considered 'excommunicated' or 'suspect' or 'heretical' or 'smorgasbord' believers are, in many ways among the most intense Christians of our time. They do more than sing in the choir or raise money for the parish center or fix flowers for the church. They care about it and call it to be its truest self. They question it, not to undermine it, but to strengthen it. . . . They do not dismiss the need for the spiritual life. They crave it. What's more, they look for it in their churches. But they crave more than ritual. They crave meaning. They look for more than salvation. They look for authenticity and the integrity of the faith. . . . They try harder to provide for themselves the kind of fullness of the spiritual life their churches fail to provide, or even deny . . . They reach out everywhere to everything that will provide new insights, new awareness of the presence of God."[18]

Author Dan Dick finds that many misfits' concerns are what he calls "holy discontent." Their expressions of discontent, he points out, are very different from what he calls "toxic influence." Toxic influence comes from church members who work behind the scenes to poison people's minds against new ideas, changes, innovations, and new people in leadership, and to undermine the authority of elected leaders and working groups.[19] In contrast, the members who feel holy discontent are advocating new ways of thinking that we need to bring out of hiding and put to use or at least give serious consideration.

Even when misfits' anger makes other church members uncomfortable, welcoming them and listening to them is important for the church. Many of their observations go to the heart of what the church is supposed to be about, if we measure that by what Jesus taught and demonstrated. Some of them may be speaking for God.

---

[18]Chittister, *In Search of Belief* (Liguori, MO: Liguori Publications, 2006), 9.
[19]Dan R. Dick, *Vital Signs: A Pathway to Congregational Wholeness* (Nashville: Discipleship Resources, 2007), 22–23, footnote; also April 11, 2007 e-mail to author.

IV

All Different, All Needed

MISFITS AND FITS CAN be a mystery to each other. We sometimes even see each other as enemies. That's not helpful either to the church or to us as individuals. If we can understand each other and see some of the reasons for our differences, we may be able to work together for our own good and the good of the church and the world.

In many ways, we misfits appreciate the fits and even wish we could be like them. They do a lot to keep the church wheels turning. Also, most of them seem happy doing it. Typical church activities evidently allow or even help them to do what they believe Christians are supposed to do. Typical worship services and Sunday School classes apparently suit their tastes and meet their needs. Taking part in church activities lets them feel good about themselves and their church. Typical church activities let the fits be with friends, too, and that seems especially important to them. One wrote me, "I find it so good just to be surrounded on Sunday mornings by all the other people in our congregation. That's all I really need from worship." Because the fits find these activities so satisfying, they're often cheerful and optimistic when they're at church. They're pleasant and genial, even fun.

WAYS THAT SEEM GOOD BUT AREN'T ALWAYS GOOD

Aren't those good ways to be? "Yes," we misfits readily admit. We want to be liked, too, and we like being with friends. We like harmony and cheerfulness and optimism. We want to feel good about ourselves and our churches. We'd like to feel as pleased with everything about the church as the fits seem to be. For years I managed to keep myself mostly convinced that I did feel that way. Yet we misfits can't avoid also saying "But those aren't *always* good ways to be." Keeping the wheels turning isn't a good thing at all if the vehicle is going in the wrong direction. We misfits get very concerned when the fits don't seem to be giving much thought to what destination the church seems headed toward or what route it's taking. We feel compelled to object when we think some of the fits' unquestioning ways are harming the church.

And we misfits like being with friends, but that's nowhere near all we need from worship services. We also feel the need for content that seems consistent with what Jesus taught and did. We need what we hear to make sense in terms of what we've learned from other apparently reliable sources of information. But hearing statements in church that contradict what they've learned from medicine or science or the daily news doesn't seem to bother the fits. In fact, they often seem unaware that any such contradictions exist. That baffles us misfits.

What especially mystifies me is that the fits don't even seem aware of what's actually being said by the words used in worship services. They evidently don't see anything odd about calling a worship service "contemporary" even though its songs and prayers use seventeenth-century words. Maybe the comfort they get from the words' familiarity is simply more important to them than what the words say. Or maybe the emotion expressed makes them feel so good that nothing else matters. The many who love the hymn "Amazing Grace," for example, evidently feel comforted by singing about God's "amazing grace that saves a wretch like me." Maybe in calling themselves wretches they feel they're practicing the humility that being a Christian requires, so seeing themselves as wretches feels good to them. But seeing oneself as a wretch seems psychologically unhealthy to me, so I cringe inwardly when I hear people gleefully singing those words. I feel like a misfit.

NOSTALGIA AFFECTS US DIFFERENTLY

For many fits, nostalgia evidently cancels a lot of what the words say. A hymn the fits have sung since childhood brings tears to their eyes, especially if it reminds them of a beloved, long-deceased family member. It makes them exclaim, "Wasn't that a wonderful service!" as they leave the church sanctuary. But I don't react that way. The fact that I loved certain people and they had wonderful qualities doesn't mean they didn't also have blind spots that I now recognize and want the church to avoid. And my having loved those people doesn't make me love everything they loved. My father loved the hymn "In the Garden," but it portrays God in a way I can't connect with, so I don't love it even though I loved and admired my father. To me, loving my father and loving his favorite hymn are totally separate.

Another difference I often see is that what the fits see as conflict in the church seems very disturbing to them, while to us misfits it is merely hearing a variety of views, which we consider valuable. I'll never forget the Sunday School class friend who suddenly stopped attending. When I asked why, she said, "I couldn't stand all that conflict." I was amazed. "What conflict?" I wondered. I hadn't been aware of any. Our class had recently started discussing some topics on which members didn't all agree, but to me that had made the class interesting for the first time. Before that, we'd merely been hearing familiar, well-loved scripture passages and sweet devotionals, with members responding, "Isn't that wonderful!" To me that had made class sessions pointless and uninteresting.

WHAT MAKES THE DIFFERENCE?

Why do fits and misfits see things so differently? Age is a big reason. Many younger people feel like misfits in church activities that many older churchgoers find comfortable. Today's younger people live with technology that's unfamiliar or even annoying to older people. They live full, fast-moving lives, so they're not interested in adding any activities that don't look enjoyable or useful. In their daily work, many have been trained to think in business terms—long-term planning, strategies, vision, bottom-line performance and progress—and they rarely see this kind of efficiency emphasized in churches.

People of all ages, however, react differently to the church because their personalities are different and they're at different points in their faith journeys. Personal differences like these often contribute to our seeing the Bible differently, seeing God differently (including the relationship of God to Jesus), and having different expectations of the church.

• The Bible

We differ in our understanding of what kind of book the Bible is. We therefore have very different opinions about how to interpret what it says.

Many misfits notice how similar the Bible is to the writings that other religions consider sacred. We're likely to be reasonably aware, too, of how much is unknown about the origins of the Bible's contents. We're also at least somewhat aware of how error-prone and politically-influenced the process was, through which these contents reached their current forms. We misfits therefore don't see the Bible's individual words as sacred, especially the words of any one translation. We don't see Bible verses as statements from God. We may see them as God-inspired, but we recognize them as human and thus imperfect efforts to connect with the sacred and understand the world. And we see the Bible as only one of many such human efforts.

Except in the most general sense, misfits don't see Bible verses as rules for how all humans should behave in all times and all situations. Instead, we see scriptures reflecting to a great extent the times and cultures in which they arose. Thus we are unconvinced by Christians who base beliefs on isolated verses and apply them to situations very different from the situations to which they originally applied.

We misfits are baffled, too, by Christians who claim that some scriptures are God's rules for all time but others in the very same section of the Bible are not. It makes no sense to us, for example, when Christians cite Leviticus 18:22 as evidence that homosexual practice is sinful, yet ignore Leviticus 19:19, which forbids wearing two kinds of fabrics in the same garment and hybridizing plants by planting two kinds of seed in the same field.

Like me, most of the misfits I hear from discount the Bible's statements about human beings and the universe that contradict today's best thinking about the natural world. In the centuries since the documents that make up the Bible were written, much has been discovered about the cosmos, about human illnesses and body functions, and about our natural environment. For the Bible's words to be convincing to us, we misfits need to see that they are compatible with these discoveries. Much that we read in the Bible seems incompatible, therefore valuable only as a memento of earlier times. It's like one of the Wright brothers' planes we might see in a museum. It's important to preserve and appreciate, but it's not useful for travel now.

We misfits wonder, too, why the fits seem to consider the Bible God's last word on all subjects, despite claiming to believe that God still speaks today through the Holy Spirit. Theologian Val Webb wonders that. She finds it odd when Christians act as if God no longer does anything as important as what the Bible describes. "Why," she asks, "are stories on the last page of the Acts of the Apostles more sacred than events that took place the following week?" In her view, "we are all inspired people." Therefore claiming that the Bible is the only or the final story negates what the Bible itself promises—that the Spirit continues to work. Webb thus concludes, "We need to distinguish between words of Scripture that can become outdated, and the Word encountered both in ancient stories and today."[20]

But to the fits, it seems, making such statements makes us misfits baffling annoyances at best. At worst, it marks us as dangerous heretics who need to be driven out of the church or at least denied any voice in it.

• Views of God and Jesus

Misfits and fits also differ in how they see God. The misfits tend to see statements about the sacred and names for the sacred as mere human efforts to describe something indescribable. A big reason for misfits' feeling like misfits is that in church they constantly hear statements portraying the sacred as a man who lives in the sky and acts like a cosmic Santa Claus, controlling everything and arbitrarily rewarding some people and punishing others. We misfits simply don't find that a believable description of God.

Many misfits are also dismayed by seeing church members believing things about Jesus that the misfits feel can't possibly be true—that he was physically born of a virgin, for example, and that he is somehow literally God's son. Some fits justify such beliefs by quoting the scripture "All things are possible with God" (Mark 10:27), but to misfits that's begging the question. It's simply a way to avoid thinking. And we certainly don't see such things as necessary to believe in order to be Christian. United Methodist pastor Leroy Howe calls insistence on such beliefs "the morass of over-belief that threatens the church's vitality everywhere."[21]

Episcopal priest Barbara Brown Taylor also expresses concern about the church members she sees mired in that morass— members who feel pressured to believe church doctrine that

---

[20]Val Webb, *Like Catching Water in a Net: Human Attempts to Describe the Sacred* (New York: Continuum, 2007), 187–188.

[21]Leroy T. Howe, in George M. Ricker, *What You Don't Have To Believe To Be a Christian* (Austin: Sunbelt Eakin, 2002), back cover.

doesn't match their experience of God or their observations about the world. Before she stopped pastoring congregations, she writes, "I had spent hours talking with people who had trouble believing."

"For some," Taylor explains, "the issue was that they believed *less* than they thought they should about Jesus." They felt sure that virgin births and bodily resurrections didn't happen, "but they had suffered enough at the hands of true believers to learn to keep their mouths shut." She found that others felt sure there was *more* to God than what they'd been told, yet they, too, felt they had to keep quiet. "They found themselves running into God's glory all over the place, including places where Christian doctrine said that it should not be." People had experienced God, they told Taylor, in a Lakota sweat lodge, in a sacred Celtic grove, at the edge of a Hawaiian volcano, and in dreams and visions they were afraid to tell anyone about. "These people not only feared being shunned for their unorthodox narratives," she saw, "they also feared sharing some of the most powerful things that had ever happened to them with people who might dismiss them."

"If it is true that God exceeds all our efforts to contain God," Taylor asks, "then is it too big a stretch to declare that coming together to confess all we do not know is at least as sacred an activity as declaring what we think we know?"[22] Many of us misfits ask this. Yet many fits are saying, in contrast, that we misfits are under-believers and therefore should be ignored, silenced, or even ousted.

Presumably the fits feel hurt and threatened when some of the beliefs that they consider essential, like the virgin birth and bodily resurrection of Jesus, are dismissed or denied by the misfits. They therefore strike back in self-defense, just as the misfits strike back when they feel pressured to accept something they find unbelievable. Each group feels hurt when its cherished beliefs are rejected by the other group. Because we feel so strongly about

---

[22] Taylor, 110–111.

our beliefs, we try to defend them, often without realizing how we're hurting the Christians who don't share them.

Trying to let us misfits know why we don't believe the right things, fits sometimes tell us, "it's because you don't really know God" or "it's because you don't know Jesus." To us misfits, that feels like a slap in the face. To us, such statements merely mean "you don't picture God in the same way I do." That's very different from not knowing God. We misfits feel sure that no way of picturing God can be completely correct or give a complete description of God. We recognize, too, that different people experience the sacred in different ways. So to us, for anyone to claim that he or she knows God but someone else doesn't seems unthinkably arrogant. It is unkind as well as unrealistic.

• *Expectations of the Church*

The third big difference I see between fits and misfits is in what they want from the church. Besides coming to church in order to be with friends they enjoy, the fits seem to come mainly for reassurance that what they believe about God, Jesus, and the Bible is correct. They apparently want reassurance, too, that their current way of behaving is okay. At least, they want to be reassured that even if it's not *totally* okay, it's good enough that they can at least count on going to heaven when they die. And from the church, they apparently want a soothing refuge from the stress of daily life. They don't seem willing to be urged to change, unless it's in a vague, relatively easy way like being nicer to the people they encounter.

The fits also seem to have a big desire for predictability. In worship services they want to know what's coming next. They want the service to have the same parts Sunday after Sunday. And they want the songs, creeds, and corporate prayers to be ones that they already know and can therefore sing or say without any effort.

In contrast, a lot of us misfits would be delighted if something unexpected happened when we went to church. We'd like to get new insight into what God may be like and what being a Christian requires. Hearing only the same words and singing only the same songs over and over is monotonous and boring for us. We want to hear something, instead, that makes us think. Getting new information and hearing beliefs expressed in varied ways is helpful for us because it makes us think about what we believe and reevaluate it, which may give us valuable new insight. Many misfits appreciate being shown new ways of experiencing God's presence. Many also want to hear a variety of opinions about how Christian principles may apply to current issues.

We want to hear our doubts and questions honestly addressed, too, rather than treated as if they don't exist or are unacceptable for Christians to have. Many misfits want to be challenged, not soothed. We want to hear better ways of making sense of what we see happening in our personal lives and the wider world, and better ways of dealing with the problems we see.

PERSONALITIES MAKE A BIG DIFFERENCE

An eye-opening feature of my own journey has been discovering some additional reasons for the differences between fits and misfits. These differences in people's attitudes and preferences show up in all of life, not just in the church, but they contribute strongly to the differences between fits and misfits in the church. Thus our churches urgently need to take them into account when planning worship and other activities.

One big influence on why we don't all want the same things from the church and don't see things alike seems to be personality differences that apparently are innate. The most frequently used way of classifying these is a system originated in the 1940s by Isabel Briggs Myers and her mother Katherine Briggs. They based their system on the findings of Swiss psychologist Carl Jung. The Myers–Briggs system uses four pairs of characteristics to define sixteen personality types.

• *The Outer World or the Inner World*

The first pair, which the Myers-Briggs system represents by the letters E and I, reflects our way of reacting to the world around us. Extraverts focus mainly on the outer world of people, places, and things and are energized by their contact with it. Introverts focus mainly on the inner world of thoughts and feelings instead. Interacting with groups of people requires effort for introverts. They're likely to find it more draining than energizing.

For worship, therefore, extraverts are likely to want to be among people and to touch and speak to each other. They may want lots of sound and activity, too. When they want to express enthusiasm for a part of the service, they're likely to express it with applause and movement. For many introverts, however, talking with people around them during a service, especially people they don't know, is uncomfortable and distracting. Being asked to hug or hold hands is a turnoff. And applause, movement, and loud, bouncy music destroy the reverent atmosphere many introverts consider important. Quiet time for reflection during worship is important for them. Their minds are busy during such times, and their pencils may be busy, too, as they reflect by writing. But extraverts tend to think out loud instead, and to them, silence can seem like wasted, boring time in which nothing is happening.

This difference creates a problem for worship planners. Features that many extraverts consider essential are a hindrance for many introverts. Extraverts make up about 75% of the United States population, so they're likely to see what they want as what everyone wants. And understandably, if a church can provide only one style of worship it's likely to choose what extraverts prefer. Many introverts thus feel like misfits in churches.

• *The Trees or the Forest*

The Myers-Briggs system uses N and S to represent characteristics that it calls iNtuition (represented by N because I is used for introversion) and Sensing. In observing what's happening around them, intuitive people mainly see patterns. They notice the layout of the forest more than the details about its individual trees. They see in an all-at-once way that they often can't give specific reasons for. They're likely to use metaphorical, symbolic, figurative language—like "seeing the trees or the forest"—to express what they want to say.

To the people Myers-Briggs calls Sensing types, the conclusions that N people come to often seem baseless, and the language Ns use often seems meaningless. Sensing types tend to focus on details and to take in pieces of information one at a time, in order, starting at the beginning. They tend to think in literal language, not in symbols and metaphors. Touches, tastes, sounds, smells, and sights speak strongly to them.

The United States population is about 75% sensing types and only 25% intuitives. This uneven distribution therefore makes many intuitives feel like misfits. I wonder if it also contributes to so many church members' seeing the words of rituals, creeds, and scripture as literal accounts of historical events or the physical world rather than recognizing them as symbolic language.

• *Personal or Logical*

The Myers-Briggs system uses F and T to represent Feeling and Thinking, two other characteristics that heavily influence what happens in churches. F people tend to evaluate events mainly on the basis of how they affect the individuals involved, while Ts mainly want to be logical and objective. Thinking-type people are more likely to make decisions and set policies on the basis of how they will affect the most people, while Fs more often consider how the decisions will affect the particular people they know and are close to personally. I wonder if Fs are more likely to see God as a person, too.

Fs are especially drawn to personal stories, but for Ts, what matters more is likely to be whether what they hear is interesting, seems reasonable, and makes them think. To reach the Ts in our churches and among our dropouts, many of whom our worship

We have gifts that differ according to the grace given to us.

—ROMANS 12:6

services are now turning off, we'd have to start expressing our message in ways that they find reasonable.

These two traits are equally distributed in the United States population, but most churches seem to have more Fs than Ts. Thus pastors often find that when members say they especially liked a sermon, that means it moved them to tears. What Fs appreciate most in hymns and sermons may seem like mere sentimentality to Ts. If there's a shortage of Ts in churches, we can easily fail to consider their needed viewpoint when we make church decisions.

• *Open-ended or Nailed Down*

The Myers-Briggs method labels a fourth pair of characteristics with the letters J and P. J stands for Judging, but it may more accurately be called decision-making. A J person wants to decide and take action, not to keep waiting a long time for more and more information. In contrast, a P—for Perceiving, also a rather misleading label—doesn't want to close the door too quickly and miss possibilities that haven't yet come to light. Like F and T, these two traits are about evenly distributed in the United States.

WE NEED THE MISSING TYPES

If we want to reach people of all personality types and benefit from all the traits that our churches need and God provides, we must appreciate and pay special attention to the views of the types that are under-represented in our churches. Knowing that we probably have fewer introverts and that they aren't likely to speak up as readily as extraverts, we need to ask them about their worship needs. Knowing that we may have a disproportionately small number of Ts, in our fear of hurting anyone's feelings we must be careful not to ignore the need for reason, logic, and efficiency that is so obvious and so important to Ts.

The combination of S and J traits creates a temperament strongly oriented to tradition, history, obedience to official authority, and adherence to standard operating procedures. These features are prominent in the institutional church just as in every large institution, so it's not surprising that many people with this temperament are drawn to it. Thus in the church we need to make deliberate efforts to listen also to members and to outsiders of other temperaments that are likely to be under-represented. We need to hear from the people who recognize new trends that are influencing the church. We need to hear from the people who focus more on the future than on the past. We need to hear from those who see the need for experiment, innovation, nonconformity, and change.

People of the less-common personality types are especially likely to feel like misfits in the church, so it's important to hear from them as well as from people of the more common types. Above all, it's important to help people of all personality types find opportunities for real community, for ministry that uses their gifts, and for worship that lets them recognize and respond to God's presence. Several nearby churches can sometimes join to provide the kind of worship services, studies, and discussion groups that people of the less-plentiful personality types need.

STAGES OF FAITH MAKE A DIFFERENCE

Another big reason for diversity of views among Christians is that they are at different stages of the spiritual journey. If we're growing as Christians, we keep moving through different stages of faith as we go through life. They are like successive levels on a spiral path that goes around a mountain repeatedly as it goes up the mountain. We keep reconsidering some of the same issues over and over, but each time they arise we see them somewhat differently from the ways in which we've seen them previously. Our path keeps leading us into new territory, and as we get higher on the mountain we keep getting a wider view than we've previously had.

When we get to new parts of the path we may see God in new ways and thus may change our ways of thinking about God, speaking to God, and experiencing God. That means some of our previous ways of worshiping may no longer work for us. As we reach new stages of the journey, we may need new kinds of spiritual food and new guides and traveling companions, too.

CLIMBING THE MOUNTAIN OF FAITH

James W. Fowler, an Emory University professor, describes stages of faith that are like successively higher levels of the mountain. He is a Christian but his stages don't just apply to Christian faith or even religious faith. They describe not *what* a person believes, but rather *how* he or she arrives at his or her beliefs about life and applies them.

Fowler warns that the stages he describes aren't a scale for measuring persons' worth. Neither are they educational or therapeutic goals toward which to hurry people. He claims that people can find wholeness and integrity at any stage. Fowler's descriptions, however, can help us see why different churchgoers may need different kinds of worship services. They can also help us see what other activities churches need to provide for people at different stages.[23]

• *Stages 1 and 2—Infancy and Childhood*

Fowler believes we begin the faith journey as infants, in a pre-stage in which seeds of trust, courage, hope, and love are planted. Then thought and language bring what he calls Stage 1. In Stage 2, a person adopts beliefs and moral rules and attitudes but interprets them literally. People at this stage see the world as based on fairness. They see God as having personal, physical, bodily characteristics. They use stories and myths to explain experience.

---

[23]James W. Fowler, *Stages of Faith: The Psychology of Human Development and the Quest for Meaning* (New York: HarperSanFrancisco, 1981/1995).

Stage 2 typically comes in elementary-school years, and some adults remain at this stage.

• *Stage 3—Keeping the Package Closed*

James Fowler finds, however, that at adolescence most people move to Stage 3. They start thinking about how they experience life. Religious people recompose their picture of God, starting to see God as having inexhaustible depths and being able to see into the depths of themselves and others. They see authority as being outside of themselves. Their main authorities are custom and tradition, valued face-to-face groups like friends and family, and the holders of official leadership roles in traditional institutions, such as pastors.

Stage 3 people don't examine and thus can't really explain the system of beliefs and values to which they are committed. It's just there, like water for fish. Stage 3 people see their faith system as a total package. They don't separate or even examine its parts. They defend their beliefs and values and feel them deeply, but they don't analyze them. And they see their faith as being everyone's faith and tying everyone together.

Stage 3 people don't separate the symbols and rituals of their faith from what those symbolize. Worthy symbols are themselves sacred for Stage 3 people. For Stage 3 patriots, for example, their nation's flag is equivalent to the nation itself, so if someone burns or spits on the flag, it's seen as an attack on the nation and thus needs to be punished and prohibited. Stage 3 Christians may consider damaging a Bible—the physical book—a sacrilege because it seems to be an attack on Christianity or even on God. Stage 3 Christians may feel that failing to take Communion in what they see as the proper way is failing to obey God.

Many adult Christians never move beyond Stage 3, therefore much that churches do is designed for Stage 3 Christians. And Fowler finds that in many ways religious institutions work best if most members are in Stage 3, because it's a conformist stage, a don't-rock-the-boat stage. Stage 3 churchgoers mostly feel obligated to do whatever their church asks of them. Conventional worship is likely to be satisfying and helpful for Stage 3 Christians, too. They won't feel any need to analyze what the words or rituals mean or to question what's being done. They're likely to see changes or even questions as denials of Christian belief or as offenses against God. They're likely to feel like fits, not misfits.

• Stage 4—Taking It All Apart

Some people eventually feel the need to leave Stage 3. Something motivates the fish to leap out of the fish tank and look at it. They may see clashes between authorities they've depended on. They may start realizing that Mother wasn't always right about everything or that what their priest says about God isn't necessarily true. A common motivation for leaving Stage 3 is leaving home, emotionally or physically or both. Reaching midlife often triggers this change. So does a big change in an important relationship or job. Whatever makes people suspect that their beliefs don't match what they see of the world, or makes them see that their ways of coping no longer work, can be the impetus for moving to Stage 4.

This move can be frightening, disorienting, and painful. It's a time of feeling cut loose from one's moorings but not seeing any safe place to move to. It can make the changing person seem strange and threatening to family and friends who haven't felt any need to change. It's thus a hard transition to make, and many people don't make it. If it happens, it's an upheaval, Fowler finds, and it can last for several years.

A crucial part of moving to Stage 4 is ceasing to rely on external sources of authority and relocating authority within the self. The Stage 4 person no longer sees himself as merely a composite of the roles he fills, such as father, doctor, or pastor. He no longer lets his identity be defined only by other people. And unlike Stage 3 people, Stage 4 people think critically about their system of meanings and values. They no longer merely accept it without question.

Stage 4 people see the meaning of symbols as separate from the symbols themselves. They believe that if a symbol or ritual act is really meaningful, its meaning can be expressed by a definition or concept. This change in a person's way of seeing symbols can bring a feeling of loss, dislocation, grief, and even guilt. But it can bring gains, too. Deeper dimensions in the meaning of the symbols become apparent, along with a wider range of meanings.

The Stage 4 people in our midst especially need the church's encouragement and help. They need assurance that there will be a safe place to move to if they let go of beliefs that no longer make sense to them. They need assurance that they won't be rejecting God or the truth by changing their way of portraying God. They need to know that they're experiencing God-inspired growth. They need safe places to ask questions and consider possibilities. They need the companionship of other Stage 4 Christians and also of some who have moved to Stage 5.

• *Stage 5—Putting It Back Together*

Eventually the Stage 4 person may become restless. She becomes aware of what Fowler calls "anarchic and disturbing inner voices." Stories, symbols, myths, and paradoxes from her own or other traditions break in on the neatness of her faith. She starts recognizing that life is more complex than the Stage 4 logic of clear distinctions and abstract concepts can cover. She begins seeing that truth has more levels than she had previously realized. She starts the move into Stage 5, a move that rarely happens before midlife.

Stage 5 people see the interrelatedness in things. They reclaim and rework their past. They see both sides or many sides of issues simultaneously. They become willing to let reality speak for itself, instead of trying to force it into familiar categories. They see that what symbols communicate can be wider and deeper than what words and concepts can cover. The Stage 5 person, finds James Fowler, can appreciate symbols, myths, and rituals because he or she has been grasped to some extent by the depth of reality to which they refer.

This kind of faith, explains Fowler, is open to encounters with traditions other than its own. The Stage 5 person expects that truth has disclosed and will disclose itself in those other traditions in ways that may complement or correct his own. Yet at the same time, he is confident in the reality his own tradition communicates. The strength of this stage is in the ability to see and be part of one's own group's most powerful meanings while at the same time recognizing that they are relative and partial and that they unavoidably distort the divine. The Christian who is at Stage 5 needs worship, learning, and companionship that acknowledge the truths contained in Christianity while also acknowledging that neither it nor any other religion knows all about God or is the only path to God.

• *Stage 6—Seeing What Is Universal*

The very few people in Stage 6 show qualities that shake our usual criteria of normalcy. They are often seen, says Fowler, "as subversive of the structures (including religious structures) by which we sustain our individual and corporate survival, security, and significance." They often become martyrs for the visions they embody. They engage in what Fowler calls "spending and being spent" in the effort to make actual what Christians call the Kingdom of God. Stage 6 people are so rare that finding one in our church congregation is very unlikely.

SOME WANT TO SEE BEHIND THE CURTAIN, BUT SOME FEAR IT

What about the Stage 3, 4, and 5 people who *are* in our congregations and our local communities? We need to help all of them grow and make them all feel welcome. But some of them want to look deliberately at the doubts, questions, and information that churches so often keep hidden, while others desperately want to avoid looking. How can we help all of them to worship God, find real community, and mature in faith?

A *Connections* reader compared pastors' fear of revealing what's now been learned about the Bible and Jesus, and about where familiar church practices and doctrines came from, to the wizard's fear of letting Dorothy see behind his curtain in *The Wizard of Oz*. Unfortunately that's an apt comparison. We can understand this refusal to open the curtain, however, if we remember that the institutional church rewards clergy for not upsetting people.

> *Let us go on to perfection, leaving behind the basic teaching about Christ and not laying again the foundation . . .*
>
> —HEBREWS 6:1

The refusal is also understandable when we look at where many members—perhaps most—apparently are in their faith journeys. For members at the earlier stages of faith, the mere suggestion of pulling aside the curtain can feel threatening or seem sacrilegious. It certainly won't seem necessary. Yet people at a later stage find looking behind the curtain essential, and those at a still later stage may see no need for any curtain.

HOW CAN WE HELP PEOPLE AT ALL STAGES?

To serve its God-given purposes, the church must provide what's needed by people in later stages of the faith journey, not just earlier ones. It must acknowledge and affirm the stirrings that are drawing some toward a new stage. Despite Fowler's claim that wholeness can be found at any stage, we need to provide some nudges and help for moving. We especially need to connect people who are starting to move or are at the later stages of faith, so they'll have helpful and understanding companions for conversation and learning. They're especially likely to feel like misfits, because in typical churches they're less numerous than people at earlier stages, and most church activities are geared to earlier stages. Also, turning loose of previous beliefs but not yet seeing a new place to go leads to feeling like a misfit. People at this stage therefore especially need support and companionship, to reassure them that they're neither alone, sinful, nor crazy when they feel the need to ask questions and move forward. They need the church, and the church and the world need them.

TYPES AND STAGES DON'T DESCRIBE ANYONE PERFECTLY

Although many people find categories like personality types and stages of faith helpful for explaining differences in behavior, no system of categories describes anyone perfectly, because every person is unique. Besides, no one fits exactly into any classification of personality types or stage of faith, and the boundaries between categories in such systems are always fuzzy. Each of us is likely to have a lot but not all of the characteristics of a personality type, and we're likely to have a few characteristics of other types too. We may be able to see ourselves mostly at one of the faith stages that Fowler or other observers describe, but we'll still have some of the characteristics of the previous stage, and we may already have some characteristics of the next stage too. No such system completely fits anyone. It's a rough approximation at best, and some people will find it more helpful than others. So no matter how helpful any such classification system may seem, attributing too much validity to it and giving it too much importance can turn it into the kind of rigid system of rules that Jesus so firmly denounced.

That's true of categorizing people as fits and misfits, too. Even those of us who feel like church misfits in some ways are likely to feel like fits in other ways. Someone who's turned off by the church's unwillingness to consider innovative theological views may still feel a strong emotional need to keep singing the old familiar hymns. None of us are total fits or total misfits.

Even though we can't separate people precisely into rigid categories and shouldn't try to, however, it's important to help everyone we can to achieve his or her potential. It's important, too, to help the church benefit from whatever contributions any interested people can make. Accomplishing these purposes requires noticing and supporting the people who for whatever reason aren't part of the majority or the current power structures and therefore are most likely to be overlooked or rejected—the people who feel like misfits.

How can church congregations help people with various kinds of talents and callings, and people of all ages, all personality types, and all stages of faith, to grow and find ways of following their callings? And how can we help them find the companions they need for their journey? We need to keep asking those questions in our churches.

V

What Congregations Can Do

STIFLING MISFITS' VOICES, AS the church often does, seems shortsighted. Besides being unkind to the misfits, it's not likely to work. If the church feels the need to show us misfits that we're wrong, then the way to pursue that is not to stifle, oust, or shun us. Neither is it to bombard us with Bible verses, because many of us understand the Bible differently from the members who typically use that way of trying to convince us.

Instead, persuading us to change our beliefs would require openly discussing with us the pros and cons of our beliefs and also of official church policies and majority views. It would require showing us convincing evidence that the church's doctrines and practices made more sense and produced better fruit than our beliefs. But of course that approach would be risky. It could cause some churchgoers to be converted to our views instead of converting us to theirs. I suspect that's why the church so often stifles new information and insight and discourages open discussion.

CHANGES WILL BE NECESSARY

How can the church be sure to hear from its misfits instead of losing what they can contribute ? Only by making some changes, many of which will have to come from the fits and from pastors.

Do not be conformed to this world, but be transformed by the renewing of your minds, so that you may discern what is the will of God—what is good and acceptable and perfect.
—ROMANS 12:2

Blessed are you when people revile you and persecute you and utter all kinds of evil against you falsely on my account.
— MATTHEW 5:11

Above all, both lay members and pastors will have to start saying openly and often in their churches that failing to conform to majority views and customs is okay. We must make clear that it's more than okay, in fact—that it's often necessary for following Jesus. The Bible is full of evidence of that.

We'll have to say it in more than one way and in many places. Not only in sermons and study groups, but also in church business meetings and in conversations, we need to say regularly that following the teaching and example of Jesus requires being different from the world around us in certain ways. Following Jesus can require breaking rules and customs, failing to meet some of our families' and friends' expectations, speaking against some of what our governments do, and even opposing some of what our churches do.

THEY WON'T AUTOMATICALLY SHOW UP OR SPEAK UP

Besides saying this regularly in words, we need to make it known by our actions, especially by including people with a variety of views in our church decision-making groups and other church activities. That means making deliberate provisions for hearing diverse views in these groups. We can't just assume that members with minority views will automatically show up or volunteer their views. If their church experience has led them to think that their views will be ignored or, worse, used as ammunition to hurt them, they're not likely to show up unless they're given convincing evidence that this won't happen.

I read a telling example of this way of dealing with minority voices in an article about NASA's failure to anticipate what had caused a space vehicle to have a fatal accident. After the accident, a NASA employee said he had seen the potential danger but had been ignored when he mentioned it during the design phase. An investigator therefore asked a project manager, "How do you seek out dissenting opinions?"

"Well, when I hear about them . . . ," she started answering, but the investigator interrupted. "By their very nature you may not hear about them." So the project manager switched gears: "Well, when somebody comes forward and tells me about them . . ."

"But what methods do you use to *get* them?" the investigator asked. The manager had no answer.

Unfortunately our churches often operate like that, too. We want only "team players" on staffs and committees. That's likely to mean only people who will go along with whatever the pastor or committee chairpeople want, or will follow official church policy without questioning it. We want only cheerleaders. We ignore the need to include critics and questioners. They can be a nuisance. They can cause conflict, which makes a lot of church people uncomfortable. Having to hear from dissenters can make meetings last longer. Yet from what the gospels tell us about Jesus, he doesn't seem to have been a team player. Instead, he bravely spoke up even when he opposed the majority or the religious leaders. And he often opposed them. He was a misfit.

In our churches, therefore, we need to hear a variety of interpretations of the Bible and a variety of views about how

Whoever comes to me and does not hate father and mother, wife and children, brothers and sisters, yes, and even life itself, cannot be my disciple. Whoever does not carry the cross and follow me cannot be my disciple.
—LUKE 14:26-27

Peter and the apostles answered, "We must obey God rather than any human authority."
—ACTS 5:29

Christian principles apply to current issues, even the controversial ones—especially the controversial ones, in fact. We need to hear from people who consider war unacceptable, not just from those who consider it permissible or even necessary. We need to hear both from those who think we need to build a wall between the United States and Mexico and from those who think it would violate what the Bible says about being hospitable to aliens.

ASK A MISFIT TO LUNCH

We need to hear from the misfits who show up in our churches, but equally important is hearing from those who have dropped out or come only rarely. And they're the ones that lay Christians, rather than pastors, may be most able to reach. Through work, school, social events, and leisure activities, lay members tend to have access to nonchurchgoers that pastors don't have. They can sometimes speak nonchurchgoers' language better than pastors can. Besides, some people hesitate to express their real views to pastors. They don't want to be seen as ignorant about the Bible or as not pious enough, to hurt the pastor's feelings, or to feel embarrassed about not attending church regularly.

Since I stopped participating in my congregation a few years ago after having been extremely active in it for nearly fifty years, only one congregation member has asked me why I stopped. The change has been very painful for me, and getting the impression that no one in the congregation cares enough to ask me why has made it even more painful. This experience has made me ask myself, however, whether I ever contacted fellow members who stopping coming, to find out why they had stopped. To my chagrin, I've realized that I rarely did that. Now I realize that I needed to do it, and then, if I saw that the missing members had been mistreated, to speak out to church leaders and other members on their behalf.

So especially if you're a fit in your congregation, I urge you to get in touch with some of its misfits. Find out firsthand from them why they feel like misfits and what has led them to views that differ from yours. Don't just depend on hearsay. Ask a misfit to lunch, and share your views with each other. If what you learn leads you to think that your church is mistreating the misfit, or to feel that it needs to give more attention to his or her views or concerns, speak up. Speak to your fellow church members and especially to the congregation's lay and clergy leaders, and keep speaking up until you see change.

USE WORDS CAREFULLY

What the church does with its opportunities to communicate with misfits is crucial. What we say in worship services, newsletters, advertisements, websites, and other official communications needs to avoid using all-masculine words for God and for human beings, for example. By calling God a member of one of the two groups of human beings—men—as churches so often do, we're saying the other group—women—is inferior. In addition, using all-masculine words when we mean both men and women makes many women feel they're being declared invisible or inferior. It makes them feel like misfits. This one-sided use of gender language turns off or even drives away many misfits, both male and female.

Also, attenders who are not married or not heterosexual can be turned off by constant references to family in announcements about church activities. Talk about "our church family" during worship services is also a turn-off for people who don't know what's being talked about and thus don't feel like part of the family. References to staff members or congregation members without explaining who they are can make visitors and newcomers feel like misfits. And this is so easy to avoid. It's so easy to say, "sign up for the dinner with our church secretary, Mary Smith," and then have Mary stand so everyone can see who she is. But so often we merely say, "turn in your registration to Mary," or worse, "everybody knows Mary," when in fact only long-time,

super-active members—the insiders—know Mary. We also make
people feel like misfits by making announcements in ways that
make sense only to the few people who are totally familiar with
the church organizational structure. This, too, is easy to remedy.
All it takes is a sentence or two: "The Charge Conference will
meet immediately after the service. In this denomination, that
is the top official decision-making body of each congregation,
elected yearly."

SHARE SPIRITUAL-JOURNEY STORIES

An especially important way to help misfits feel welcome is to
let stories of spiritual journeys be heard openly and often. We
need to hear accounts of members' and pastors' spiritual journeys
regularly in worship services, church-school classes, and other
church gatherings. However, these accounts need to come from
both fits and misfits. We need to hear a variety of experiences and
viewpoints, not just the views and experiences of people whose
backgrounds and beliefs match those of the majority.

Hearing how the spiritual journeys of both fits and misfits
have led them to their present views can increase fits' and misfits'
appreciation of each other and willingness to participate in the
church together, along with helping the misfits feel welcome.
Hearing these accounts can help both fits and misfits to see some
reasons why different Christians have different beliefs about the
Bible and the church.

Sharing spiritual-journey stories resembles what used to
be called "giving testimony," but it differs in an important way.
Scholar Diana Butler Bass reports that "testimony" is one of the
traditional Christian practices she found used by thriving United
States mainline Protestant churches. We hear a lot about the need
to "walk the talk"—to act on what we say we believe—but Bass
reminds us that "talking the walk" is very important too. We need
to let others know what experiences and information have led
us to our present beliefs. However, this doesn't mean giving the

kind of testimony that has negative connotations for many older Christians. When they think of testimony, many recall rambling, predictable, jargon-filled accounts that made them groan and roll their eyes. These older Christians recall endless-seeming stories of someone's "accepting Jesus and being saved" at age five, or stories of other conversion experiences that happened decades ago and apparently were the end of the testifiers' spiritual growth. What Bass is referring to instead, and I'm referring to in recommending that we share spiritual-journey stories, is sharing stories that tell of continuing spiritual growth and of faith journeys that keep leading to new and often unexpected places.

"The entire New Testament is a testimony," Bass reminds us, "a record of experiences that early Christians had with the transformative power of God. Those early believers wrote down their testimonies, their experiences of sharing their testimonies, and the impact of their testimonies on the people around them. This basic structure underlies almost every book in the New Testament."[24]

HEAR SHORT VERSIONS AND LONGER VERSIONS

Few worship services are long enough to include more than one abridged spiritual journey story. However, if that account is carefully composed, it can be extremely helpful even if it is very short. And in other settings in which more time is available, such as retreats, church-school classes, or study groups, hearing fuller versions can be appropriate and helpful.

One way of reflecting helpfully on one's spiritual journey privately or describing it to others when time is not severely limited is to draw a time line to represent one's lifetime. Peaks and valleys in the line represent the events that have especially felt like ups and downs. Another way is presenting one's story as if it were a book's table of contents, giving titles to the book and its

---

[24]Bass, 134.

individual chapters. Still another helpful way is describing one's "spiritual ancestry" by using a genogram drawing. It's the kind of drawing that counselors sometimes use to help a client recognize behavior patterns or hereditary physical conditions that keep reappearing at all levels of the client's family tree. For more about this method, see the July and August 2000 issues of *Connections*, on my website, *www.connectionsonline.org*, or for still more, see a book I co-authored, *Spiritual Family Trees*.[25]

USE CONTEMPORARY CONTENT, NOT JUST CONTEMPORARY METHODS

To attract many of the misfits I hear from, worship services would need to have up-to-date content. Many churches offer what they call contemporary worship services, but too often only their technology and musical styles are contemporary. Their words are far from contemporary. To make more of us misfits willing to sit through services, they would need to use today's English. The words of their songs and prayers would need to reflect today's best understanding of the universe. Sermon topics would need to reflect the best recent findings about the Bible and ways of portraying God. They also would need to include suggestions about how the teaching of Jesus may apply to today's most pressing world issues or to problems currently being experienced by the local community.

BE INCUBATORS, NOT ABORTIONISTS

Another important way for congregations to furnish the support misfits need is by helping them pursue ministries to which they feel called. Those are likely to be creative new ministries, not just ministries that are already part of the institutional-church

---

[25]Larry W. Easterling and Barbara Wendland, *Spiritual Family Trees: Finding Your Faith Community's Roots* (Herndon, VA: The Alban Institute, 2001).

system. Jeff Proctor-Murphy, co-founder of the excellent "Living the Questions" video-based course, calls this kind of help being an incubator. As he was developing the new course, he reports, his congregation was very open to diversity of people, ideas, and viewpoints, and its lay members had a high level of commitment. They tested the course's materials and sponsored public talks by the scholars who appeared in its videos. The congregation was an incubator for its pastor's innovative project.

All congregations need to be incubators. They need to be safe, nurturing settings for the ministries to which its members find God calling them. That's especially true when a ministry involves expressing minority views, exploring new insights, or doing something that hasn't been done before.

Unfortunately, however, some congregations are abortionists instead of incubators. They try to kill members' newly-conceived insights and ministries. I heard about one such congregation recently from a layman who has been its victim. He's been in the same church denomination all his life, and for years he worked almost full-time in his congregation without pay. He's loaded with talents, skills, commitment, and other resources that the church urgently needs. But now he has decided to leave.

He has been concerned for a long time, he explains, about the church's failure to address glaring social-justice issues. "In the 1950's," he wrote me, "I couldn't help wondering why black kids had their own schools in my hometown. I also thought it was unfair for the black kids and Mexican-Americans to have to sit in the balconies of our movie theaters."

"Where was my church during all this?" he asks. "Going along to get along. Fitting in. Not making waves." And he sees today's church doing that now with regard to current injustices. He doesn't see it speaking up about war policies that in his view contradict the teaching of Jesus. He doesn't see it willing to risk criticism and loss of members by letting people of all sexual orientations participate fully in the church. "I want something more," he writes, "so in a few weeks I will quietly resign my membership in an organization in which I have never felt I completely belonged. I regret that I could not do more to help the church during my years of leadership participation."

I hate to see the church lose this man. And I fully understand his frustration in trying to carry out the ministries to which he strongly feels God calls him, in a congregation that doesn't welcome his talents or support his efforts. I feel sad every time I'm reminded of forward-looking pastors and lay members whose congregations have not only refused to support their efforts but in many cases have actively opposed them. And being aware of these tells me that there are many more like them whom I'm not aware of.

AVOID WAYS THAT AREN'T LIKELY TO WORK

An important part of making misfits feel welcome is recognizing that some ways in which churches often try to attract them aren't likely to work.

Appealing to feelings of obligation isn't likely to motivate misfits. If they have never been part of a church or have already dropped out or lessened their participation, that shows that they don't see church participation as their duty.

But actually we're misrepresenting the Christian faith and life if we present it to anyone, misfit or not, mainly as a duty. Some religious practices can be helpful, but being Christian doesn't mean being obligated to observe any particular religious practices, even those that the majority of Christians observe. I like the way in which early-twentieth-century Catholic priest and scholar Pierre Teilhard de Chardin expresses this. "Christianity is not, as it is sometimes presented and sometimes practiced," he wrote, "an additional burden of observance and obligations to weigh down and increase the already heavy load, or to multiply the already paralyzing ties of our life in society. It is, in fact, a soul of immense power which bestows significance and beauty and a new lightness on what we are already doing."[26]

---

[26]Teilhard de Chardin, 70.

DON'T RELY ON FEAR OF HELL

Fear of going to hell isn't likely to persuade church misfits, either. We misfits tend to see terms like heaven and hell very differently from the way in which a lot of the fits see them. The misfits I'm most aware of see heaven and hell as symbolic terms that don't refer to actual places. To these misfits, claims about heaven and hell and "being saved" in the sense of where one goes after death simply don't hold water. They contradict everything that is now well known about the universe. In fact, hearing Christians' claims about being saved and going to heaven is a big part of what makes us feel like misfits. So we aren't likely to be convinced by being told that "believing in Jesus," accepting official church doctrines, or participating in a church is necessary in order to avoid going to hell. Such claims just turn us off.

PERSUASIVE HINTS FROM PASTORS

To make misfits feel less like misfits and show them that what the church offers is credible and worthwhile, pastors could help through their sermons and conversations. They could at least include hints that the ways reflected in the most familiar hymns, creeds, rituals, and other parts of typical worship services aren't the only ways of seeing God or Christianity or the Bible. Pastors could give at least tiny suggestions that the words of these parts of the liturgy can't be interpreted literally and that they raise legitimate questions. The hints might need to be subtle to keep from driving away the members who can't bear to learn that their beliefs may not be totally correct. But even a tiny, subtle hint is big enough to be picked up by a misfit who is looking for one. Even a tiny hint would let members who don't share the majority view know that at least one person in the congregation—the pastor—recognized that other views were possible and permissible. It would also let misfits know that the pastor might be available to talk with them about other views. It could let them know that he or she might even be open to the possibility of introducing a few new activities into the church program, to interest the people who now feel like misfits.

PROVOCATIVE STUDIES AND BOOK DISCUSSIONS

What kind of activities? One I've discovered is the "Living the Questions" study course I mentioned above, created in 2006 by two United Methodist pastors. It features thirty presenters on a DVD that provides about twenty minutes of video to open each session, plus a few pages of related material for participants to read in advance. The presenters are from a variety of church denominations and ethnic backgrounds. They have forward-looking understandings of Christianity. They provide the kind of up-to-date information that many churches provide little of, about the Bible, Jesus, and Christianity. They also stimulate helpful discussion about important aspects of these topics.[27]

Book discussion groups can also appeal to many people who now feel like misfits. If a congregation had a member who read books that dealt with questions of belief or with current social-justice issues, he or she might be glad to lead such a group. If the group were well publicized, not just within the congregation but also in the wider community, it might attract other misfit book-readers who had thought they were alone.

OFFER VIEWS AND INFORMATION TO CONSIDER, NOT INDOCTRINATION

To appeal to many of the people who now feel like misfits, however, we need to make clear that any study courses or book discussions we offer will be presentations of information and opinions for attenders to consider and come to their own conclusions about, rather than efforts to make them believe church doctrine.

---

[27]For more information about this course and others offered by the same group, see www.livingthequestions.com.

Some Christians feel that indoctrination is the very thing we need to be doing, of course. They make fun of people who they think treat the Ten Commandments as if they were only the Ten Suggestions. But how we interpret such scriptures depends on whether or not we see the Bible's exact words in our favorite English translation as having come straight from a person-like God. In presenting our interpretations of scriptures, therefore, we need to be careful to say, "This is what I believe God requires of us," or "This is what most of today's Christians believe," instead of claiming that our favorite verses present facts or are God's commands simply because they're in the Bible.

Especially when we publicize Bible study groups and other church activities outside of our congregations, we need to make clear that freedom in interpreting scriptures and doctrines is permissible. And outside our congregations is where such activities need to be publicized in order to attract many of the people who feel like misfits. Unfortunately, though, we're rarely willing to risk letting a variety of interpretations be presented in our study groups or to say that there's more than one Christian interpretation of Bible verses. *Connections* readers sometimes tell me about unofficial book-discussion groups they're part of but don't feel safe in mentioning within their congregations. Painful experience tells members of these groups they'd be criticized for being in a group whose members have views that differ from the majority or from official church doctrine. A member of one such group tells me, "We meet in a dark corner of the church basement, and hardly anyone knows we're there." Another says, "We gain so much from the books we read, but we can't mention them out loud in our church."

A friend told me about his experience in a congregation that doesn't want minority views heard. In one of its Sunday School classes, he said he didn't think the United States should be involved in the current war in Iraq. The next day, the class teacher phoned him and told him not to come back to the class unless he would avoid bringing up controversial subjects like that. The class had a policy, she reminded him, of not discussing controversial subjects or saying anything critical of the church. He later recalled, however, that he had often heard support for the Iraq war expressed in class. What this meant, he realized, was that the class policy didn't actually require avoiding controversial subjects. It only required not expressing any view that differed from the majority's view about a controversial subject.

Hearing this friend's account, I wondered, "Aren't controversial subjects the subjects we most need to be discussing in the church?" And don't we need to be hearing a variety of views about them? If we all have the same opinion about how Christian teachings apply to a current issue, why discuss it? The most fruitful discussion includes several views. It looks at what seem to be the pros and cons of each one. So our churches not only need to *allow* a variety of views to be heard. We need to *invite* many views. And we need to address the tough, controversial issues, not just those on which most members agree.

AVOID HOSTILE MESSAGES

Someone recently commented to me, "Of the books currently on the best-seller lists, four are by atheists, and the only people who aren't reading and talking about them seem to be the people in churches." That's unfortunate. Even if we think these authors are wrong, how can we effectively show where they're wrong without having accurate information about what their views are and why they hold them? And how can we expect them to consider our views seriously if we are merely bad-mouthing theirs?

Here's what one of those best-selling authors, neuroscientist Sam Harris, writes in his *Letter to a Christian Nation*, a tiny, easy-to-read book that I wish every Christian would read despite disagreeing with some of Harris's views. "Since the publication of my first book, *The End of Faith*," Harris reports, "thousands of people have written to tell me that I am wrong not to believe in God. The most hostile of these communications have come from

Christians. This is ironic, as Christians generally imagine that no faith imparts the virtues of love and forgiveness more effectively than their own."[28]

How can we expect people to find our beliefs convincing if the behavior that results from them is hostile? One of the most obvious and most important but most often overlooked ways to make misfits feel welcome in our churches and communities is to treat them with compassion rather than with hostility.

Another important way is to present Christianity in a way that makes sense to them.

---

[28]Sam Harris, *Letter to a Christian Nation* (New York: Random House/Vintage Books, 2008), vii.

VI

What Misfits Want to Know

To find christianity credible, many misfits must be convincingly shown that Christian beliefs make sense. Trying to get us to believe things that seem to contradict everything we experience and observe isn't likely to get anywhere with us.

To see Christianity as believable, we feel the need to know what has been discovered about the earthly life of Jesus in recent years. And if that doesn't seem to match what the gospels say, then we want to know why the church expects people to believe only the gospel versions. Also, when statements in the Bible don't seem to match today's best thinking about human beings and the rest of the natural world, we want to know why the church keeps presenting those parts of the Bible as timeless truth.

Many misfits are put off by seeing that in all other areas of life Christians require evidence before believing claims about what the world is like or what is happening in it, but not in the area of religious belief. We're amazed by Christian doctors, for example, who use the very latest discoveries in their medical practice but base their religious beliefs only on what was known in the third century or even many centuries earlier. Scientist Sam Harris is one who finds this kind of behavior baffling. "Tell a devout Christian that his wife is cheating on him, or that frozen yogurt can make a man invisible," Harris observes, "and he is likely to require as much evidence as anyone else, and to be persuaded only to the extent that you give it. Tell him that the book he keeps by his bed was written by an invisible deity who will punish him with fire for eternity if he fails to accept its every incredible claim about the universe, and he seems to require no evidence whatsoever."[29]

To reach many of the misfits who are teetering on the brink of dropping out of the church or who have already dropped out or have never been in, the church would have to address these concerns openly and convincingly.

UP-TO-DATE INFORMATION ABOUT THE BIBLE

To be convincing to many of us misfits, evidence that the Bible is uniquely true can't come from the Bible itself. That kind of evidence doesn't prove anything. It uses reasoning that merely goes around in a circle. It says, "We know that this statement in the Bible is true because the Bible says it is." That's no more convincing than someone who says, "I'm the smartest person in the world" but can't come up with evidence that anyone else thinks he is.

To be convincing, evidence that statements in the Bible are true must come from somewhere else besides the Bible. It may come from the findings of historians, archaeologists, and other scholars and scientists. Later findings sometimes prove some of these researchers wrong, of course, and some people who claim to be Bible scholars seem to look only for what will support their views. Besides, even the most trustworthy scholars disagree, and even the most objective scholars' assumptions and expectations color how they interpret their findings. But for deciding whether a statement from the Bible is believable, considering the findings of scholars and other materials outside the Bible seems much more likely to be reliable than merely taking the Bible's statement at face value without knowing anything else about it.

---

[29]Sam Harris, *The End of Faith: Religion, Terror, and the Future of Reason* (New York: W. W. Norton & Co., 2004), 19.

Besides scholarly findings, the other source of evidence likely to be convincing to many misfits is seeing the Bible's claims borne out in personal experience. That's a matter of interpretation, of course, and every such interpretation is subjective. What seems reliable to one person doesn't to another, and different people interpret the same experience in different ways, in addition to seeing God in different ways.

Consequently, we misfits feel that we mainly need to see consistent results in order to believe claims based on personal experience. To believe that God healed a cancer patient because of prayer, we've got to see a convincing explanation for why many other cancer victims die despite having been prayed for.

Above all, convincing us misfits that the Bible's statements and Christian doctrine are believable requires explicitly and openly addressing our real doubts and questions. We want to hear both pastors and lay Christians admit theirs. We want to hear them acknowledge that there's no way to know all there is to know about God. We want to hear them admit that Christians don't all agree about how to follow Jesus today. We need to hear these things not only in worship services and church classes but also in our conversations with Christians.

MORE THAN SPIRITUAL SARAN WRAP

Many of the misfits I hear from also want to hear discussion of how the Bible's message applies to important current issues. We misfits want to hear pros and cons of the death penalty compared to Jesus's apparent rejection of violence and the Ten Commandments' prohibition of killing. We want to hear pros and cons of various proposed health-care systems considered in light of Jesus's commands to heal the sick. We know there's more than one Christian opinion about such issues. We want to hear minority views as well as the majority view.

Attracting more of us misfits to worship services would also require providing more of what we see as real substance. A misfit friend told me recently that she was almost ready to stop attending church. She cares deeply about the church's purpose, but, she said, "Everything in my church's worship services is like Saran wrap." I knew exactly what she meant. When you look at Saran wrap, you don't see anything. You immediately see right through it. It's flimsy. And it's uninteresting. Why spend an hour every Sunday being given the spiritual equivalent of Saran wrap?

Author Patricia O'Connell Killen describes a similar feeling expressed by a woman whose longing for God was not being fed by what she experienced in her church. She rightly suspected that the Christian heritage included what could satisfy her longing, but she never saw those parts of the heritage presented when she went to church. She said, "I feel like I'm standing by a river, dying of thirst."[30]

INFORMATION ABOUT CHURCH OPERATION

What many misfits especially feel the need to get from the church also includes practical information that churches too often keep hidden. Some of this information relates simply to how our congregations and denominations operate—how pastors are assigned, what has caused some to be ousted, and what's being done with church property and why. Because of privacy requirements, legal liability, or property-purchase negotiations, some of this can't be openly revealed, but some is concealed that doesn't need to be concealed. It's information that church members need to know and that there's no valid reason for not letting us know. The explanation "it's confidential" sometimes seems to mean merely "it's being swept under the rug to keep a church official or the church from looking bad or from having to answer hard questions about what happened."

---

[30]Patricia O'Connell Killen, *Finding Our Voices: Women, Wisdom, and Faith* (New York: Crossroad Publishing Co., 1997), 1.

We need to know such things in order to help protect the church from leaders' wrong actions. But above all we need to know in order to be real parts of the church body rather than mere spectators. We need to be informed in order to be able to contribute informed opinions, suggestions, and actions that will help the church follow its calling and not stray from it.

Besides information about routine church operations, the church's shortcomings also tend to be kept hidden, and many lay Christians, especially the misfits, see that as dishonest. Like the class members who told my friend their class prohibited bringing up anything critical of the church, many church members see criticism of the church as taboo. Explains Roman Catholic priest Richard Rohr, "some fear all critical thinking because they fear the structures will collapse." Others apparently feel that criticizing the church would be like criticizing God—definitely not a permissible thing to do. But in Rohr's view, which I share with him and many other misfits, "there is such a thing as healthy criticism. People who love something have also earned the right to make it better and keep it true to its deepest vision. . . . When you recognize that you are an accomplice in the evil and also complicit in the good, and take responsibility for both, when you can use the language of 'we' and not 'them,' then . . . your criticism is coming from love, not hate."[31] It's the truth-speaking that New Testament descriptions of the church urge members to do, as in Ephesians 4:15.

More than just information about church problems and shortcomings needs to be made known to members, however. Information about what decisions congregational decision-making bodies are considering, and even the names of the members of those bodies is sometimes unavailable to church members who don't belong to them. Lay members who feel left out with regard to church operation want to know when major decisions are

---

[31]Richard Rohr, *Hope Against Darkness: The Transforming Vision of Saint Francis in an Age of Anxiety* (Cincinnati: St Anthony Messenger Press, 2001), 170.

due to be made by church staff or decision-making bodies, and they want to know while there is still time for their views to be taken into account. The church therefore needs to ask openly for members' views about upcoming decisions. After the decision is made, church leaders need to make known that these views were seriously considered and if possible, why they were rejected if they were rejected.

PASTORS ARE AFRAID

Information about church operation is far from the only kind of important information that's kept from members. It's possible to be active in a church for years without learning some of the main facts about Christianity. It's easy, in fact. Information that scholars and other church observers have known for decades gets to very few churchgoers, yet some of it could help all of them see more clearly what following Jesus really requires.

Much of what church members need to know about the Bible, Jesus, and Christianity has been known for years and presented in good-quality seminaries for years. Pastors who have been to first-class seminaries and who stay informed after they graduate know much of this information. Why, then, don't churchgoers hear it regularly in sermons? Why not also in church-school classes and Bible-study groups? Fear seems to be the main reason.

Some pastors fear that if they revealed what they've learned about the Bible and church history, it would keep some people from joining their churches. It would also cause many current members to leave, because it would reveal that some of their beliefs were not true. If many members left, those pastors would look bad. They might soon be out of a job. At best, they'd get moved to churches that paid less and had less prestige. Understandably, few pastors are willing to risk that.

Pastors also have other reasons for limiting what they reveal, however. Every pastor presumably feels called by God to lead people to Jesus Christ and help them become more faithful followers of Jesus. Giving them too much information too soon, many pastors fear, can be like trying to make members take adult steps in that process when they are only ready for baby steps. It might drive them away before they were ready for further growth or before they could even see the need for it.

CONCEALING WHAT HAS LIBERATED AND STRENGTHENED THEM

Jeff Proctor-Murphy sees the fear of pastors and regrets its effects. A big part of what motivated him to create the "Living the Questions" course was seeing how fearful most of his fellow clergy were. He saw that for them as for him, the findings of biblical scholarship they had learned in seminary had been liberating and faith-strengthening. But unlike him, they weren't sharing these findings with the members of their churches. They were afraid it would drive people away. Proctor-Murphy was dismayed by this. He felt strongly that if these findings had been so helpful for the pastors, they were cheating their members by not offering the same help to them.

Eric Elnes made a similar observation when he met a woman who had been "protected" in this way by her pastor. Elnes wanted to tell her that her pastor in fact had never been a real pastor to her. "In twenty years," Elnes wanted to say to her, "he's never told you what he really thinks is important. He's never stretched your thinking. He's never moved you to look beyond yourself to really embrace your neighbor. He's never offered you the ecstasy of discovering a God who is so much bigger and more gracious and loving than you ever imagined. He's never trusted you enough to have an authentic relationship with you or your congregation." But instead of saying that to her, Elnes reports, "I replied, 'How nice.'" Then later, he regretted not having had the nerve to let her know what he really felt.[32]

---

[32]Elnes, 113.

I wish more pastors gave members the benefit of the doubt by assuming that many would welcome the newly discovered information and expanded images of God that the pastors themselves have found helpful. But unfortunately, many members who want more information stay silent and passive instead of actively supporting brave pastors. Thus these silent members let the more vocal and fearful members do harm that is out of proportion to their numbers.

THE LOUDEST CERTITUDE COVERS AMBIGUITY

The big problem with concealing information in the church is that what drives some people away is necessary to attract others. How can the church reach the people who want full information and a variety of views in order to grow in their faith, without driving away those who are afraid of any information or speculation that makes them question their current beliefs or disillusions them about the church? Should we concentrate on those who want to grow, or should we ignore them in order to keep from losing those who don't? Ideally, we would meet the needs of both groups, but how can we do that?

If we wait until all members feel ready to move forward in their spiritual journeys, we'll wait forever. All of us occasionally need a nudge of some kind, to make us aware that there's more to discover beyond what we've already seen. A big part of the role of pastors is to furnish the nudges and tugs that motivate members to grow. A pastor's role is not to soothe us by making us think we don't need to venture into any new territory in our spiritual journeys. Neither is it to delude us into thinking that certainty is possible.

Old Testament scholar Walter Brueggemann reminds us of this. "It is the pastoral task," he believes, "to help people entertain their own ambiguity. I believe that underneath the loudest religious certitude there is characteristically enormous ambiguity. I suspect the more shrill we are at the surface, the more there is ambiguity underneath. The Spirit has the best chance for newness in our ambiguity. Therefore I think it is the pastoral task to name in a safe place the ambiguities that all of us are trying to cover up. I believe that newness arises out of those ambiguities, and our common sectarian ideologies cut us off from our own ambiguities."[33]

United Methodist professor Walt Herbert makes a similar observation. "We are all answerable for the way we read holy texts," he believes, as I also do, "and for the way we interpret moments of mystical awareness. This responsibility compels the acceptance of uncertainties that are shunned by those who seek the comforts of blind unquestioning faith. Religious authoritarians offer those comforts by pretending to certainties they do not possess."[34]

"Authoritarian religiosity, in whatever tradition," Herbert reminds us, "masks inner fears that authentic faith addresses directly."[35]

LAY CHRISTIANS ARE AFRAID

Hearing information and ideas we haven't previously been aware of is often the nudge that spiritual growth requires. So is recognizing the ambiguity that all talk about God must include if it is not to be idolatry. Why, then, do some church members leave merely because of getting such nudges? Why do some try to oust pastors who provide such nudges?

Many of these members seem to be afraid of what they might find. They're evidently afraid to find that uncertainty exists where they feel a great need for certainty. They're afraid to find out that the Bible reflects human shortcomings. They don't want to know that even in its earliest years the church included diverse beliefs

---

[33]Walter Brueggemann, in *The Prospect of a World Community of Religions: Domination or Collaboration?* (Jackson, MS: D. L. Dykes, Jr. Foundation, Faith and Reason Symposium 2005 at Millsaps College), First Plenary Presentation.

[34]T. Walter Herbert, *Faith-Based War: From 9/11 to Catastrophic Success in Iraq* (Oakville, CT: Equinox Press, 2009), 10.

[35]Herbert, 141.

and fierce political battles, yet it did. These church members apparently want the comfort of taking their favorite selected Bible verses at face value and not considering any other verses or interpretations. They want the assurance of believing that every statement in the Bible came straight from God's mouth and that all religions other than theirs are wrong. These Christians may want the certainty of thinking they already know all about God. Feeling sure that they will go heaven when they die and non-Christians won't is apparently vitally important for them. And these Christians apparently feel that the church exists to uphold and spread these beliefs.

Anything that introduces uncertainty therefore threatens to shatter these church members' security. What if they found that some of their beliefs were wrong? Might that mean they are destined for nothingness when they die? Might they find themselves without the divine help they now count on? Might they discover that being Christian doesn't give them any higher standing with God than non-Christians? Might they discover that the church doesn't have the only truth or the whole truth? Those seem to be terrifying thoughts for many Christians. For them, refusing to consider such possibilities is apparently the only bearable way of dealing with them.

UCC pastor Robin Meyers is concerned, as I also am, about the biblical illiteracy and anti-intellectualism that are so prevalent in the church because of these fears. They have caused today's church, he observes, to have theological laryngitis. He warns us that if the church doesn't start openly and actively presenting the life and message of Jesus in a more intellectually honest way, using the findings of modern scholarship, the church is likely to lose its voice even more.[36]

While many members fear learning more about the life of Jesus and the origin of familiar doctrines, however, others of us

---

[36]Robin Meyers, *Saving Jesus from the Church: How To Stop Worshiping Christ and Start Following Jesus* (New York: HarperCollins, 2009), 18.

drop out, stay away from church, or feel like misfits in it, for the opposite reason. We feel the urgent need for greater openness and intellectual honesty in the church. We feel sure that neither Christianity nor any other religion could have the whole truth or the only route to God. We see churches and individual Christians making claims that seem unbelievable in light of what science, medicine, and contact with other religions and cultures have now revealed. We see churches losing people like us by refusing to reveal the best current thinking about the Bible, Christian history, and the nature of all religions. We see that concealing this information in order to protect fearful members drives off many others.

CHAOS-TOLERANT
AND CHAOS-INTOLERANT PEOPLE

Retired United Church of Christ pastor Jack Good feels that people differ greatly in the amount of disorder they can tolerate, and I suspect he's right. I wonder if this difference is part of innate personality differences.

Jack Good believes that although most people long to press experience into shapes that make sense to them, this kind of organizing urge is much stronger in some than in others. Those who can't tolerate much chaos or uncertainty want a Bible that is the literal word of the divine, he observes. They want to see God as a power that micromanages every detail of the universe. They want a theology that was given by God in correct form to ancient church councils and is right for all times and places. They want assurance that ultimately good things will happen to good people and not to others. Thinking-oriented, chaos-tolerant people, however, aren't willing to be mere passive recipients of beliefs like these, that contradict their understanding of how the world works. These chaos-tolerant people are as hungry for a spiritual home as chaos-intolerant people are, but honesty is apparently a more essential element of the home that the chaos-tolerant seek.

In Good's view, fundamentalist churches have aimed their message precisely toward chaos-intolerant persons. These churches meet genuine needs of people who are at a particular stage of religious growth. Thus these churches grow. "Their message may stretch mental credulity at many points," observes Good, "but it is stated with clarity." Mainline churches, by contrast, try to appeal to everyone. They dilute their message in the hope of offending no one, but that means it may not strongly attract anyone.[37]

What concerns me about this tactic is that when churches limit their message to what the chaos-intolerant want, they are promoting a spiritually unhealthy way of living. They're being harmful enablers. Like giving alcohol to alcoholics or drugs to drug addicts, these churches are giving people beliefs that they want but that harm them. Churches are helping members continue in beliefs that the most recent findings about the Bible, the universe, and history seem to have shown to be baseless, such as portrayals of a flat earth with God in the sky above it and a fiery hell below it. Every Sunday, churches are being enablers by feeding people hymns, anthems, creeds, and rituals whose words make claims that in any other setting would be considered delusional if they were taken literally, which is how most churchgoers seem to take them. By continuing to use these hymns and creeds without making clear that their words can't be taken literally, we are keeping members comfortable but in a harmful way, like keeping an alcoholic comfortable by helping him or her to keep drinking. Also, by doing this we are driving other members away and giving outsiders the mistaken message that Christianity has no truth or real help to give.

AWARENESS IS THE FIRST STEP

Often the remedy for fear is information. The first step toward needed change is recognizing that something is wrong. The next

---

[37]Jack Good, *The Dishonest Church* (Scotts Valley, CA: Rising Star Press, 2003; reprinted by St. Johann Press, Haworth, NJ, 2008), 55–56.

step is seeing a change that might remedy what is wrong. It's like turning on the lights and searching when we hear a scary noise at night, and finding that the cause was merely a closet rod that fell. It shows us something that needs our attention. Cowering in bed in the dark might be temporarily more comfortable than getting up and looking for what caused the noise, but only learning the truth can bring a solution. The closet rod probably had been coming loose for some time, but until it got our attention by falling, we didn't realize it needed fixing.

The misfits who see the need for change in the church and in our understanding of the Bible and Christianity are doing members a favor, therefore, by calling attention to church shortcomings and to information about the Bible and Christian history. Misfits don't do the church any favor by keeping quiet and concealing what they see, even though that may be more comfortable for the fits, the pastors, and, in some ways, even for the misfits.

CHANGE IS SCARY

For most of us, change is scary even when we know it's necessary. The truth is often scary because seeing it lets us know that change is needed.

Change means having to start dealing with something unfamiliar. Even if our current situation is bad, we've learned how to handle it, and there's a kind of comfort in that. Change, by contrast, means venturing out into something that we don't know if we'll be able to handle. What if the unknown turned out to be worse than the known? Most change also requires going through a time in limbo before we get to the improved circumstances. While we're in that limbo, our old way of thinking is no longer available but we haven't yet found a satisfying new way. We're afraid of what we'll find if we go forward, but we can't go back. For all these reasons, change is scary and sometimes painful, so all of us often avoid it if we can.

It's like needing surgery. We may want to avoid knowing about a malignant spot if it isn't causing any pain. We hate to have to subject ourselves to surgery that we know *will* cause pain, even if the pain will be only temporary and the surgery will help in the long run. That's how the prospect of changing our basic beliefs and habits often feels. Merely seeing the need for change can be uncomfortable and scary, even if we risk serious trouble by refusing to see it. So both fits and misfits can be uneasy about change. Yet Christianity is all about change—changing ourselves and changing the world. The church's purpose is thus to promote both of those kinds of change. That means urging members to make changes even if they're scary and painful.

"In most congregations," Jack Good observes, "a shift from duplicity to honesty will cause some measure of distress. For a few individuals, the discomfort will be extreme." However, "the vast majority will do more than survive; they will grow spiritually. More than that, an honest presentation of faith might draw back some who have drifted away."[38]

WHAT IF IT SEEMS TOO LATE TO CHANGE?

Sometimes we avoid letting ourselves see new insights because we feel it's too late to put them to use. I hear pastors speak with regret about seeing only after retirement that during their active years of ministry they failed to preach and do what they now believe following the teaching of Jesus requires. It's painful to realize that when it's mostly too late to act on it.

I also see older women and men insisting that women should stay subservient to men, that for women to fill their time only with trivia is fine, that women should be shielded from life's unpleasant facts, and that they need men's help for easy tasks like opening doors. Yet I wonder if the main reason for women's and men's denying that anything is wrong with this way of living is that they have spent so many years following it, thinking that it was required. Now it feels too late to change, so the only alternative

---

[38]Good, 126.

is convincing themselves that the way they've spent their lives has been all they wanted and also what God wanted.

Some change is possible to make and important enough to make, however, no matter how late in life we are. It may be too late for some of us to set out on new careers, but it's almost never too late to change at least a few of our ways of thinking and acting.

A note I got recently from a ninety-one-year-old retired clergyman reminded me of that. "Just in the last five years," he told me, "have I begun to raise the basic questions. It is the common belief that as you grow older you grow more conservative, more willing to let it go undisturbed. I have found the opposite to be true." He admits that the changes he's making fill him with mixed feelings. "Have I wasted my life espousing a 'gospel' which now I see as false or severely compromised?" he asks himself. "Do my new insights give me any sense of comfort or assurance?" But he answers that last question with a definite yes. "I feel like I am in transition and don't have much longer to figure it all out. But with all the uncertainties this transition exposes me to, I am glad, so very glad, that I have waked to a fresh and more promising view. I feel like the gay man must feel when he comes out of the closet for the first time. That feeling is made more intense living as I do in the very heart of rank conservatism. Keep going in your quest for truth."

LEARNING ABOUT THE BIBLE

Ways in which we find we need to change, even late in life, often include our ways of seeing the Bible, because knowing about the origin and nature of the Bible can have big effects on how we act. If we keep seeing the Bible verses forbidding same-sex relationships as God's rules for all time, we will treat gay people cruelly, violating the teaching of Jesus. If we base our views about war on Old Testament verses describing God as commanding one group to slay another, we will fail to follow Jesus's command to love our neighbors.

Understandably, few church members are willing to learn about the Bible by reading the books and articles full of footnotes and multi-syllable words that scholars write mainly for fellow scholars. However, knowing what scholars have found can often help us make sense of what we read in the Bible. It can even help us recognize God's presence in our lives. We therefore need to become aware not only of scholars' discoveries but also of their speculations about the meaning of those discoveries.

By failing to reveal the findings of scholars, the church too often acts as if they don't exist. That contributes to making many thinking people feel like misfits. The church's refusal to reveal the very human ways in which its doctrines and sacred writings originated makes many thinking people reluctant to be part of the church. It keeps them from believing its claims and seeing the value in Christianity. If we want to be convincing to the world and to make fewer people feel like misfits in the church, we'll have to start being much more open in communicating what our best thinkers have discovered.

VII

What the Church and the World Need to Know

MANY MISFITS WOULD FEEL less like misfits if churches revealed more of the ideas and findings of today's best thinkers about the Bible and Christianity. Churches now conceal much of this information, yet it could help both fits and misfits grow as Christians. Making it known would also give outsiders a more accurate, believable, and thus favorable picture of Christianity.

An important part of the information that churches so often conceal is that in many ways the Bible is very similar to the writings that other religions consider sacred. It has unique features, of course—mainly what it says about Jesus—but the similarities are too obvious to ignore.

Christianity and the other major world religions have important similarities, too, despite their differences. Most emphasize compassion, for example, often in statements very similar to what Christians call the Golden Rule. Parts of the documents held sacred by other religions also advocate cruelty and violence and uncritically show those being practiced, of course, but so do many parts of the Bible. Some followers of other religions act violently today, but so do many people who claim to be Christians. Those who blow up abortion clinics and African-

American churches come immediately to mind. The Crusades are another glaring example, but history includes numerous others, from early centuries to very recent years. Many Christians conveniently ignore the violent parts of the Bible and the violent actions of Christians, while seeing violence as the main feature of other religions.

A GIANT TURTLE, A TALKING SNAKE, A TINY GENE POOL

I've found some of scholar Karen Armstrong's books especially helpful for learning about how the Bible originated and developed, how other religions and their sacred writings developed, and how they all reflect cultures very different from ours. I recommend *The Great Transformation: The Beginning of Our Religious Traditions*[39] and *The Case for God*,[40] both of which are thick but definitely worth the time and effort.

An important similarity between the Bible and other religions' stories and writings is that many of the Bible's contents are expressed in the same kind of symbolic language that fills the writings and stories of other religions. Like the other writings, for example, the Bible contains creation stories that seem to be efforts of early civilizations to explain what they observed. None of these stories can be taken literally as science or history.

I remember seeing in Canada a beautiful wooden sculpture of the giant turtle than one native tribe portrays as the beginning of all that exists. It seemed preposterous to me at first, but then I realized it was no more preposterous than the talking snake that plays a leading role in one of the Bible's accounts of creation. Taking either the Bible's story or the Canadian tribe's story literally is what's preposterous. Both are ancient cultures' legends expressed in metaphorical language.

---

[39] New York: Alfred A. Knopf, 2006.
[40] New York: Alfred A. Knopf, 2009.

A friend told me about his daughter's reaction to hearing Adam and Eve presented in her Sunday School class as if they were literally the first two human beings. "There would have been a really small gene pool if that had happened," this perceptive eleven-year-old commented. But why should we be surprised at such a reaction? If we don't present the Bible in ways that acknowledge what even children now know, we can't expect to be taken seriously. Instead, we can expect many well-informed, thinking people of all ages to feel like misfits in our churches or to stay away from them.

A CENTURIES-LONG PROCESS, ANONYMOUS WRITINGS

In our churches, we need to make clear that the Bible as we know it today grew out of centuries of oral tradition, in cultures very different from ours. The Bible reached its present form through a centuries-long process in which separate and unrelated documents were written, copied and recopied, lost, found (often centuries later), collected, edited and re-edited, and translated and retranslated. And today we have none of the original documents—none. All that has survived, as far as anyone knows, is copies of copies of copies. Some were apparently made by copiers who didn't know the language—even the alphabet—of the documents they were copying, and many copiers did their copying in dark rooms by candlelight. Imagine how easy it would have been in these circumstances for a character to have been accidentally replaced by a different character, changing a word into a completely different word.

Besides, the writers, collectors, editors, and translators of the documents have had varied motives for doing what they did. In choosing what documents to include and how to combine them, they understandably chose what would support their views. Early Christian communities had significant differences, so one writer's or compiler's views often differed from another's. And when several words seemed equally likely to express the meaning of the original, later translators apparently chose on the basis of what they thought the document should say. Later research sometimes makes those choices look like they misrepresent the original meaning, but so much later and in a different culture, it's hard to be sure. Considering the original context in which a scripture was written is important, yet figuring out what that context was is often an educated guess at best. Because of the many uncertainties and opportunities for error in this long process, basing a belief or behavior today on a mere few words of a particular Bible translation seems extremely unwise. But we rarely hear that acknowledged in church.

In fact, we sometimes even hear it denied. Here's how a *Connections* reader in a mainline Protestant congregation recently described such an experience to me. "The leader of my class argued for a precise definition of a word in a scripture passage. I said we can't know for sure because we don't have any original scriptural documents. The leader told me I was wrong. I asked our associate pastor to reassure her that what I had said was true. She listened to me and suggested I visit the Unitarian Church across town. I have effectively been excommunicated."

I'm often astonished by what I hear from devotees of a popular nondenominational Bible study. "We don't use any commentaries or interpretations," they boast. "We study only the Bible's words." That's an outrageous claim. Making that choice—to consider "only the Bible's words"—is making an interpretation. It's interpreting the English words of a translation as having come straight from God and as being the only words God ever said or ever will say. It's claiming that taking those words literally, at face value, and learning nothing about where they came from tells us all we need to know about their meaning. Given the complex process by which the Bible reached its present forms, this way of interpreting it is grossly misleading. We need to hear that regularly in church.

UNKNOWN AUTHORS

Another problem in interpreting the Bible is that the authors of many of its books are unknown. The main exceptions are some of Paul's letters. The Bible's anonymous authors include the writers of the gospels and several of the letters often attributed to Paul. Names of notable followers of Jesus and Paul were apparently attached to those writings as a way of saying that they expressed what certain early Christian communities understood to be the meaning of Jesus and the views of Paul. That apparently was standard practice in the ancient world, not what we now call forgery or plagiarism.

Also, scholars find that few books of the Bible were composed by just one person at one time. Several include sections that come from different authors and different time periods. This is evident to scholars from the inconsistencies between what different sections say, and from ways in which writing styles differ in different sections of the book.

NO ONE LIST OF BIBLE BOOKS

Along with all these uncertainties about the Bible's sources, there's no agreement on which books make up the Bible. The Bible versions used by different branches of Christianity and different church denominations include somewhat different lists of books. No one list was ever officially adopted by the whole church, and there are no universally accepted answers to the question of which books belong in the Christian canon. The term "canon," which comes from Greek and Semitic words meaning a measuring stick, is now used to mean a particular group's standard for its faith and identity. A list of New Testament books was first referred to as a canon in 367, but even then, the issue of which books belonged in it still wasn't settled for Christians in other locations.

All these characteristics of the Bible make me strongly feel that we must base our beliefs only on its overall message and how that message seems to relate to today's best thinking about history, the universe, and human beings. We can't reasonably base beliefs on only a few isolated Bible verses or even any one list of what the Bible includes. The more we discover about how it developed and how history and culture influenced its content, the less basis we have for claiming that it presents the only true religion or the only route to God or heaven. We certainly can't legitimately claim that the Bible gives us timeless rules spoken by God. And the diversity in scholars' interpretations as well as those of lay Christians gives us even more reason to avoid seeing any scripture or any interpretation as a unique or timeless statement from God.

Like many other thinking Christians, theologian Val Webb believes that "attempts to twist ancient experiences into timeless rules must be challenged, as Jesus challenged the rules in his day." She also believes, as I do, that we must protest when Christians insist that some ancient laws are valid today but others are not, as when Christians quote Leviticus to oppose same-sex relationships but ignore Levitical prohibitions on blood sausage. "When the Bible (or any sacred text) is used to encourage hate, oppress human beings, incite violence against humanity or the earth, or to demand we leave our minds and experience at the door," Webb writes, "it behooves inspired or Spirit-breathed humans to go back to that text and liberate it from those who use it in inappropriate, noncompassionate ways."[41] We need to hear this message regularly in church.

NO FIRST-HAND REPORTS

Besides being uncertain about so many overall aspects of the Bible, we're really unsure of a lot about Jesus. No book of the New Testament was written during his earthly lifetime. The gospels aren't what we now know as biography or history. When Jesus

---

[41]Val Webb, *Like Catching Water in a Net*, 189.

spoke and acted, no one was present taking notes. At least, no such notes have turned up so far. And none of the Bible's accounts of Jesus were written by what we would now call an objective writer. They were all written by his devoted supporters. The only report we have about Jesus that was written during his century by a nonfollower is a very few sentences by a Jewish historian named Josephus.

The earliest writing in the New Testament is apparently one of Paul's letters to the Thessalonians, and it wasn't written until about 50 CE, about twenty years after Jesus died. Matthew, Mark, and Luke were apparently written about 70 CE, and John even later, about 90. ("CE" stands for Common Era—another bit of information that often goes unexplained in the church despite being unfamiliar to many members. Only one out of every three humans on earth is a Christian, so in recent years many have come to feel that CE and BCE are more appropriate than A.D.—Latin for "in the year of the Lord"—and B.C., for "before Christ.")

Several descriptions of incidents in the Bible's four gospels are inconsistent with each other and with some of what has now been learned about that period from archaeology and other historical sources. Besides, these four weren't the only gospels. Fragments of several others have been found and published in relatively recent years.

For all these reasons, it is unreasonable to treat every feature of the gospels as history or to assume that the statements they present as direct quotes from Jesus actually came from his mouth. In the church we need to be made aware of this and frequently reminded of it.

JESUS WASN'T A BLUE-EYED BLOND BORN ON CHRISTMAS

Jesus wasn't born on December 25 in the year 1. Apparently no one knows the exact day of his birth, but based on related events reported in the gospels and in historical documents, scholars believe he was born at some time during the year that today's calendars call 4 BCE. What's more, the celebration that we now know as Christmas was originally a secular festival—one that most of today's Christians would call "pagan." Our celebration of Easter also grew out of a secular festival, and the exact day of Jesus's death is unknown. We need to be reminded of these facts regularly in church, too.

Neither typical Christmas pageants and carols nor Holy Week observances give a historically factual picture of the life of Jesus. They merge events from all four gospels as if they all happened at the same time, and they ignore the question of whether the Bible's descriptions of these events are literal or metaphorical. They also distort each of the gospel stories, as well as how the events would have had to be related in time if they had happened.

Another misleading aspect of how Jesus is usually presented is that he undoubtedly didn't have light skin or European facial features. This should be obvious, given what we know about where he lived, but most of the pictures on our church walls and in our heads deny it. He probably looked more like Osama bin Laden than like our most familiar Jesus pictures, but our churches rarely make this apparent.

THE MAIN CONCERNS OF JESUS WEREN'T JUST SPIRITUAL

The gospels show Jesus constantly fighting injustice and using political tactics to oppose the oppressive system of his time, yet today's church often gives the impression that he was concerned only with heaven and with personal spiritual concerns and personal behavior, especially sexual behavior.

Several contemporary Christian thinkers are now speaking up about the need to stop presenting Jesus as what one of them, African Methodist Episcopal Church clergyman Obery M. Hendricks, Jr., calls "the meek, mild Jesus who told us, in a nice, passive, sentimental way, to love our enemies." This Jesus, Hendricks observes, is "a gentle, serene, nonthreatening Jesus whose only concern was getting believers into heaven," but it isn't the Jesus the gospels describe.[42] We definitely need to hear this regularly in church.

THE INFLUENCE OF THE ROMAN EMPIRE

An especially important factor in understanding what Jesus said and did is that he spent his entire life in a part of the Roman Empire. Many of his words and actions were responses to oppressive features of this all-pervasive system. Its army was continually visible throughout the area in which he lived and did his ministry. Its taxes caused the peasant class of Israel, to which Jesus belonged, to live in poverty. Its brutal methods of punishment dealt cruelly with anyone who became burdened by insurmountable debt or who openly defied the authority of the emperor and his agents, as Jesus did. "Son of God" and "savior," which Christians think of as referring exclusively to Jesus, were common titles given to Roman emperors. Ancestors of Augustus, the emperor when Jesus was born, were said to have been led to Italy by a star, and when Augustus died, the Roman senate decreed his ascension into heaven. So applying these titles and stories to Jesus was a denial of the emperor's authority, not a statement about biology or history. As theologian Joerg Rieger points out, "what sounds like purely religious terminology to modern ears could be heard as a subtle challenge of the Roman Empire."[43]

"GIVE THE SPIRIT SOMETHING TO WORK WITH"

Jewish New Testament scholar Amy-Jill Levine gives an example of a scripture that shows Jesus opposing the Roman Empire but that often isn't recognized as referring to the Empire. Her

---

[42] Obery M. Hendricks, Jr., *The Politics of Jesus: Rediscovering the True Revolutionary Nature of Jesus' Teachings and How They Have Been Corrupted* (New York: Doubleday/Three Leaves, 2006), 1–2.

[43] Joerg Rieger, *Christ and Empire: From Paul to Postcolonial Times* (Minneapolis: Fortress Press, 2007), 32.

example comes from the story in Mark 5:1-20, about Jesus driving "unclean spirits" into a herd of pigs. "The story . . . allows a nice political dig against Rome," Levine explains, "given that the 'unclean spirits' identify themselves as 'Legion,' the Latin term for an army cohort."[44]

Some Christians say they don't need to know such information, but Levine disagrees. She tells how she responds when her students insist that they don't need to know the historical and cultural settings of Bible passages. Students tell her, "I read the text and the Holy Spirit guides me," but she doesn't accept this as a valid reason for staying uninformed. She advises them, "Give the Holy Spirit something to work with."[45] We need to hear that from our churches.

Jesus actively subverted and resisted the Roman Empire in numerous ways. Ignoring this fact gives us the wrong impression of what being one of his followers requires today. It lets us avoid seeing the need to oppose empire as it shows up in today's world—to oppose what Joerg Rieger calls the "large and ever-changing conglomerates of power that are aimed at controlling all aspects of our lives."[46]

"Empire," explains Rieger, "has to do with massive concentrations of power that permeate all aspects of life and that cannot be controlled by any one actor alone. . . . Empire seeks to extend its control as far as possible; not only geographically, politically, and economically . . . but also intellectually, emotionally, psychologically, spiritually, culturally, and religiously. . . . Empire displays strong tendencies to domesticate Christ and anything else that poses a challenge to its powers."[47]

Because most of today's empires aren't based on formal colonialism as the Roman Empire was and more recent empires such as the British Empire have been, empire is hard for us to

---

[44]Amy-Jill Levine, *The Misunderstood Jew: The Church and the Scandal of the Jewish Jesus* (New York: HarperSanFrancisco, 2006), 25.
[45]Levine, 7.
[46]Rieger, vii.
[47]Rieger, 2–3.

recognize in today's world. As Marcus Borg and John Dominic Crossan point out, "empire is not intrinsically about geographical expansion and territorial acquisition. . . . Rather, empire is about the use of superior power—military, political, economic—to shape the world as the empire sees fit. In this sense, we are the new Rome."[48]

WE OVERLOOK THE ROMAN EMPIRE'S INFLUENCE

Our empire is also hard for us to recognize, Rieger observes, because empire's structures are less visible now than in the days of the Roman Empire.[49] Empire's pressures are more overpowering now, but it rarely has uniformed soldiers visibly stationed in our midst. It is all-pervasive, but more often through advertising rather than through calling its leaders sons of God. Christians therefore tend not to notice the presence of empire in today's world, even if they realize that Jesus actively opposed it in his world and that we need to oppose it in ours.

References to the Roman Empire in the New Testament are especially likely to go unrecognized by Christians who, like me, aren't scholars. I never realized until I heard Marcus Borg speak and then I read his and Crossan's book *The Last Week*, that Jesus is likely to have been expressing deliberate resistance to the Roman Empire when he entered Jerusalem on the day we now call Palm Sunday. "Two processions entered Jerusalem on a spring day in the year 30," Borg and Crossan speculate on the basis of recently-found ancient artifacts and documents. "One was a peasant procession, the other an imperial procession. From the east, Jesus rode a donkey down the Mount of Olives, cheered by his followers. . . . On the opposite side of the city, from the west, Pontius Pilate . . . entered Jerusalem at the head of a column of imperial cavalry and soldiers. Jesus's procession proclaimed the

---

[48]Marcus Borg and John Dominic Crossan, *The First Christmas: What the Gospels Really Say About Jesus's Birth* (New York: HarperCollins, 2007), 238.
[49]Rieger, 314.

kingdom of God; Pilate's proclaimed the power of empire." Jesus's group apparently was making what we would now call a planned political protest demonstration, but we're likely not to realize that, because the Bible doesn't make the contrast of the two processions explicit.[50]

If Borg and Crossan are right about what Jesus's procession was like, our typical Palm Sunday observances deliver a very different message from the one that his procession delivered. Many of our churches have little children re-enact it, greeted by delighted exclamations of "Aren't they cute!" from adult churchgoers. Yet to be faithful to the original procession's intent, we would evidently need to have a procession of church members carrying signs along the nearest Interstate highway or our town's Main Street, expressing opposition to current imperial policies of our governments—policies that contribute to poverty, promote war, or deny civil rights to certain groups, for example.

Many Christians feel the church should strictly avoid using political methods, yet Crossan, like numerous other scholars, assures us that our distinction between what is political and what is religious would have been meaningless to the Jews, pagans, and Christians of the first century. Much of what we see as Christian religious language, Crossan points out, was the political language of public discourse in Jesus's world. To follow Jesus, therefore, we would have to get more involved in what we think of as political issues. In our churches we would need to have political conversations openly and often.[51] But instead, many church members complain vehemently if their pastors say anything these members consider political. Others are actively trying to get rid of their denomination's agencies that are authorized to use political methods to oppose empire and injustice on behalf of the denomination.

---

[50]Marcus J. Borg and John Dominic Crossan, *The Last Week: A Day-by-Day Account of Jesus's Final Week in Jerusalem* (New York: HarperSanFrancisco, 2006), 2, 4.
[51]John Dominic Crossan, "Mysticism, Empowerment, & Resistance."

UNCONVENTIONAL VERSIONS CAN HELP

Part of what keeps us from noticing how we need to be applying Jesus's teaching and the tactics of the Old Testament prophets to our current conditions is that our setting is so different from what we read about in the Bible. For this reason I find books helpful that speculate about what Bible passages might say if they were written today in our culture. A favorite of mine is *The Unauthorized Bible,* by Gary Holthaus. Its title reminds us that translations and interpretations of the Bible's contents don't have to be authorized by any official group in order to be helpful guides for following Jesus.

In Holthaus's compelling poetic version, Jesus's parable of the poor Lazarus who meets a rich man in Hades becomes the story of Arnold, a rich employer of migrant workers, and Miguel, a worker who lives with sixteen other men in a trailer that has no potable water. Miguel's job includes spreading chemical fertilizers and pesticides that are labeled with warnings in a language he can't read. Holthaus's picture of this pair is frighteningly familiar.

> Arnold the businessman
> has his friends over on Sunday
> after church. They feast on
> roast beef, fresh vegetables.
> bountiful salads, desserts a la mode.

> When Arnold has a toothache
> he goes to the dentist.

> When Arnold's wife stubs her toe,
> she goes to the doctor.
> When Miguel's hands begin to peel,
> he keeps on working.
> When Miguel's wife miscarries,
> they stop the bleeding with towels.

Miguel and Arnold die of cancer and meet in the afterlife, where Miguel rests under leafy oak trees with his water jug while a parched Arnold gasps in the hot sun.

"If this is the way
the system really works,"
Arnold croaks, "Can you at least
send Miguel back
to warn my brothers?"

But the Foreman answers,

"You and your brothers
made much of Sunday church.
. . .
If you all
did not believe then,
your brothers will never
believe a man like Miguel."[52]

Holthaus's Jesus is a little man who drives a '74 Ford Pinto that keeps needing repairs with makeshift parts to stay running. Some Christians see such portrayals of Jesus as offensive, but to me this portrayal is entirely appropriate and in fact is one of *The Unauthorized Bible*'s most valuable features. It presents an impossible-to-miss contrast to the glamorized Jesus pictures that so many of us have in our heads and on our church walls. It is consistent with the Bible's decidedly unglamorous description of the "suffering servant" (Isaiah 53:2-3), which our churches often claim is a portrayal of Jesus.

A CULTURE-SHATTERING RULE BREAKER

Texas pastor Rick Diamond also reminds us how unconventional Jesus was, in contrast to our usual assumptions about him. "He

---

[52]Gary Holthaus, *The Unauthorized Bible: Selected Readings* (North Berwick, ME: BW Press, 2003), 47–52.

isn't interested in anyone's rules or ideas," Diamond observes. "He is immoral in the very best sense of the word. . . . Jesus broke every rule and moral code he could find. . . . He did not behave." Diamond reminds us that "he committed every kind of blasphemy. . . . He believed that the ultimate blasphemy was to say you know the right answer." His teachings, finds Diamond, were "radical stuff. Culture-shattering. . . . If Jesus' plans come true, no institution that is based on rules and regulations can remain standing."[53] Diamond isn't advocating anarchy here. Rather, he is suggesting that top-down institutions based on inflexible rules don't seem likely to promote the kingdom Jesus sought to establish.

Catholic priest Richard Rohr, too, warns us how far we have strayed from what Jesus apparently was like. "Jesus consistently undoes historic religion," Rohr writes, "by touching and consorting and doing the 'impure' things."[54] Says Rohr, "Christianity, for many, has come to mean anti-intellectual, fanatically narrow-minded people."[55] He assures us that real Christian faith is radical and scary, therefore rare. "Religious group-identity," he observes, "becomes its most common replacement. Then we don't have to find and live from a positive and loving place. We can just go to church."[56] He feels that the cross has become merely "our company logo,"[57] when it actually was "the price that Jesus paid for agreeing to live in a 'mixed' world that was both human and divine, bad and good, simultaneously broken and utterly whole." In Rohr's view, "He lived fully on the horns of the human dilemma and made it work for us. In fact, he said it is the 'only' way. It is in that sense only, that Christianity is the 'only' way to be saved."[58]

---

[53]Rick Diamond, *Wrestling with God* (Lake Mary, FL: Relevant Books, 2003), 148–149.
[54]Rohr, 28.
[55]Rohr, 15.
[56]Rohr, 26.
[57]Rohr, 21.
[58]Rohr, 34.

OUR DOCTRINES AND TRADITIONS AREN'T ALL
FROM THE BIBLE OR THE EARLY CHURCH

Besides needing to hear information about the Bible's origins and the life of Jesus, in the church we also need to hear how familiar Christian doctrines originated. Many members assume that they're all "in the Bible." However, many of the most familiar and widely accepted doctrines aren't stated in the Bible. Instead, they were developed by church leaders who lived several centuries after Jesus.

The main description of the role of Jesus that we hear in today's churches is the theory of substitutionary atonement. It says that Jesus, who was sinless and thus didn't deserve any punishment, let himself be killed or that God let him be killed as a substitute for other humans, who unlike him are all sinful and thus deserve severe punishment. The result, according to this theory, is that all who declare themselves followers of Jesus are saved from the punishment they deserve: going to hell when they die. In today's church, through the words of familiar hymns and other parts of worship services, we're constantly given the impression that this meaning of Jesus's role is a fact. We're led to assume that it comes straight from the Bible and is the only true explanation of what Jesus did and still does for us. We get the impression that somehow the blood of Jesus saves us from going to hell when we die. However, this interpretation is actually only a theory and is only one of several theories about the role of Jesus.

In the form in which we now hear the substitutionary atonement theory, it was first presented by Anselm of Canterbury, a theologian and Archbishop of Canterbury who lived more than a thousand years after the death of Jesus.

Some contemporary Christian theologians find this theory unbelievable because it portrays God as an abusive parent, which God surely wouldn't be. Episcopal Bishop John Shelby Spong calls it a neurotic aspect of our worship, an obsession with guilt and the need for punishment.[59]

---

[59]John Shelby Spong, *The Sins of Scripture: Exposing the Bible's Texts of Hate to Reveal the God of Love* (New York: HarperSanFrancisco, 2005), 170–171.

However, theologian Joerg Rieger observes that this view, which presents God as a tyrant with arbitrary power, fails to take into account the logic of empire. It ignores Anselm's way of seeing God as the ultimate ruler at the top of a hierarchical society. For Anselm, explains Rieger, sin was the violation of God's honor, and honor was about the relationship between lord and vassal. It ordered society and made possible relationship in general. In Anselm's view, Rieger believes, humanity needed to make an act of satisfaction to restore God's honor, meaning the relationship of God to God's creation. But only God could make a satisfaction proportional to the sin. The satisfaction was thus made by the voluntary death of the God-human, Jesus. Through his death he earned a reward that he passed on to humanity. According to Anselm, Jesus's death was not the appeasement of an angry God but the restoration of the order of the world.[60]

TIME TO EXPLAIN

It's unreasonable to expect this much explanation or this diversity of views to be presented in a worship service to explain the theory of substitutionary atonement. However, we need to know that it is a theory, not a fact; that it is only one of many theories about Jesus's role; and that like other church doctrines it reflects the culture in which it arose. We also need to know that different Christians see it differently. Too often instead, we merely sing hymns about being "saved by the blood of Jesus" without even being nudged to think whether that is a credible explanation of Jesus's role or being reminded that it arose many centuries after Jesus's death.

Our churches need to let members know the meaning and origins of other familiar belief statements, too. The word "trinity" is not in the Bible, for example. In fact, the doctrine of the Trinity, which many Christians today consider essential, didn't originate until the fourth century. And what we know as the "Apostles'

---

[60]Rieger, 125–146.

Creed" did not originate with the original apostles. It reached its present form in the fourth century, when it developed as an effort to combat various views about the meaning of Jesus. The doctrine of "original sin" also arose long after the time of Jesus, with Augustine.

THE LOSERS BECAME KNOWN AS HERETICS

Hearing how these doctrines originated makes many of us misfits question their credibility. In many cases, doctrines' official adoption by church councils came after fierce political debate and power struggles. Reading about the ancient church councils that formulated now-familiar doctrines, I can't help thinking about the fiercely political denominational decision-making bodies I've been part of. Their decisions seem to depend mainly on which political bloc manages to overpower another, and I doubt that ancient church councils were any holier than this.

As Barbara Brown Taylor reminds us, being classified as a heretic in the early church merely meant coming out on the losing side of some of these political battles. "When the bishops had finished crafting a central confession of Christian faith," she explains, "people who did not choose this option became known as heretics," a term that comes from the Greek word for "choice."[61]

More than most of us realize, the early church actually included quite a bit of variety in its beliefs. Groups in different geographical locations, especially, had somewhat different beliefs and practices.

Many church traditions are a lot more recent than church members realize, too. Some that members assume are from the early church actually came only from eighteenth-century England or early America. Some that members consider essential—favorite methods of taking communion, for example—

[61]Taylor, 176–77.

are merely the customs that these members happen to have seen most often in the churches they've attended. Some practices members feel attached to may go back no farther than these members' childhood. They may be customary only in the part of the United States where these members happen to have lived. It's no wonder, then, that people with wider experience are turned off by seeing such customs treated as if they were Christian essentials.

Refusing to part with such a custom is like refusing to discard a gift wrapping. It may be beautiful, but it can't last forever, and its worth came from what it contained, not from the wrapping itself.

> *Then Pharisees and scribes came to Jesus from Jerusalem and said, "Why do your disciples break the tradition of the elders? . . ." He answered them, "And why do you break the commandment of God for the sake of your tradition?"*
> —MATTHEW 15:1-3

JESUS DIDN'T CREATE THE CHURCH AS WE KNOW IT

In focusing on the church's "wrappings" more than the meaning of their content, we often lose track of what Jesus emphasized most. Some of today's Christians point out how far the church has strayed from his actions and teaching. George Baldwin, for example, expresses dismay that "most people are of the opinion that the Christian Church was initiated by Jesus through the formation of his small band of disciples, but that is not the case." In Baldwin's view, which many other students of Christian history share, "the development of the Christian Church emerged from the missionary endeavor of Paul."

In the view of Baldwin and some others, the influence of Paul contributed heavily to making the biblical theme of salvation the prevailing approach to understanding Christianity in our society. In this view, the emphasis on social justice and liberation that was more prominent in Jesus's ministry moved into second place and remains there still. Still other Christian thinkers, however, urge us to recognize that although Paul differed from Jesus in some ways, he was an essential part of the Christian tradition and developed some important alternatives to the status quo of his time.

Baldwin also believes, along with others, that in making Christianity the official religion of the Roman Empire, in the fourth century, "the Emperor Constantine was not converted to Christianity so much as Christianity was utilized to serve the interests of the Roman Empire." Then over time, explains Baldwin, "instead of challenging the systemic evil of the domination systems, the Christian Church accepted its role as one of the Powers and continues in the present day to hold fast to its position of privilege and influence."[62]

EVEN A SENTENCE OR TWO WOULD HELP

Pastors could help all churchgoers and also lessen the tension between fits and misfits by using some easy and quick ways of communicating at least a tiny bit of what scholars have found but few church members know about the Bible and Jesus. Pastors could help to convey at least some of this by briefly mentioning background information to introduce routine parts of worship services. These are the most frequent opportunities for pastors to reach the most church members, and only a sentence or two would be necessary if such information were given regularly.

Before reading a gospel passage, the pastor could say, "This was written many years after the death of Jesus, so we can't assume that it contains direct quotes from him, but it evidently expresses an important aspect of his teaching." Or, "scholars find that the word 'legion' in this story refers to the Roman Army." It would help, too, if before a congregation recited the Lord's Prayer the pastor said, "we don't know whether Jesus spoke these

---

[62]George W. Baldwin, *A Political Reading of the Life of Jesus* (New York: iUniverse, 2006), 57, 59.

exact words, but they express much of what many Christians have considered important for many centuries." Using a variety of translations of the Lord's Prayer during worship services would also help. It would remind churchgoers that the translation we're most familiar with didn't come from the mouth of Jesus.

Brief explanations like these would help churchgoers realize what kind of document the Bible is. Such statements would help hearers realize that Jesus addressed the political situation in which he lived—that he wasn't concerned only with personal piety.

Quick reminders about familiar creeds and doctrines would help, too. Before reciting the familiar Apostles' Creed in worship services, hearing a quick sentence or two of explanation would be helpful. "This was composed several centuries after Jesus's original apostles lived. Notice that it says nothing about Jesus's ministry, yet the gospels emphasize his ministry much more than his birth or his death."

AN EASY CHANGE TO MAKE

A big part of why many thinking people feel like misfits in the church is that they feel the need for such information but don't get it from the church. They feel the need for a presentation of Christianity that is compatible with the findings of today's best scholarship.

Churches could easily provide such information if they chose to. It's a change they could put into effect rather quickly, in fact. They might lose some fearful members by doing it, but I suspect they'd gain the support of other people who would help the church come closer to its true purpose of promoting compassion and justice. Isn't that a valuable enough result to be worth trying for?

VIII

What Misfits Can Do

CONGREGATIONS NEED TO DO a lot more to make misfits welcome, but if you feel like a misfit, don't wait for that to happen. You can help yourself in some important ways.

If you're spiritually homeless and want a spiritual home, how might you find one? If you feel like a misfit in relation to the church but want to feel more like part of it, and maybe want to help the church and other misfits, too, how might you do that? How might you find the community and the kindred spirits you yearn for? I can't give any guaranteed-to-work answers to those questions, but I'll suggest some here that may be helpful.

PLANT SEEDS THAT MIGHT BEAR FRUIT

Above all, I urge you to speak up and keep speaking up. Keeping quiet merely preserves the vicious circle of silence that keeps us all feeling alone when we're really not alone. It keeps our concerns from carrying the weight they need to carry in the church. It keeps us from finding the kindred spirits whose company we wish for. Even if speaking up doesn't locate the kindred spirits you want, it may plant a seed of new insight that will eventually bear fruit for someone who hears you, so it's still worth doing. Something good may happen much later as a result of what you've said, without your even being aware of it.

I was getting a routine blood test recently when the phlebotomist who was drawing blood commented on the day's cold, wet weather. She was blaming it on God and repeatedly calling God "he." I didn't feel like starting a discussion with her about whether God had caused the bad weather. However, I felt I had nothing important to lose by making this total stranger think I was out of my mind, so I asked her, "How do you know God isn't 'she'?" The phlebotomist stopped with the vial of blood in mid-air and stared at me as if I were crazy. That probably was the end of the experience, but maybe not. She'd obviously never considered my question before. Maybe she was shocked enough by it to give it some more thought after I left. I'll never know, but I hope so.

FIND CONSPIRATORS

Sometimes mentioning one of your beliefs, concerns, experiences, or questions turns up a kindred spirit in a totally unexpected place. Years ago I read a description of that kind of encounter that I've never forgotten, by author Marilyn Ferguson. The people I think of as kindred spirits, she called conspirators, a word whose roots mean "people who breathe together."

"Brief meetings are enough for recognition," she said she had learned from a survey she had done. "Some conspirators said they sometimes relate an anecdote among co-workers or strangers and watch for a reaction, for understanding. Like the primitive Christians, . . . like a resistance movement . . . Meet them at the produce bins and [they] look like next-door neighbors who'll talk about the price of one pear and what's happening to coffee unless you share their search."[63]

Author Nikos Kazantzakis also writes about trying to find conspirators. "I strive to discover how to signal my companion

---

[63]Marilyn Ferguson, *The Aquarian Conspiracy: Personal and Social Transformation in the 1980s* (Los Angeles: J. P. Tarcher, Inc., 1980), 114.

. . . to say in time a simple word, a password, like conspirators. . . . Let us unite, let us hold each other tightly, let us merge our hearts."[64]

NOTICE PREVIOUSLY UNNOTICED PEOPLE

My all-time favorite description of finding kindred spirits comes from an early-twentieth-century Quaker, Thomas Kelly.

"A wholly new alignment of our personal relations appears. Some men and women whom we have never known before, or whom we have noticed only as a dim background for our more special friendships, suddenly loom large, step forward in our attention as men and women whom we now know to the depths. Our earlier conversations with these persons may have been few and brief, but now we know them, as it were, from within. For we discern that their lives are already down within that Center which has found us. . . . Other acquaintances recede in significance; we now know that our relationships with them have always been nearer the surface of life."[65]

Kelly goes on to describe the excitement of discovering new members of our "unofficial groups of kindred souls," in contrast to broader groups such as church congregations. "A 'chance' conversation comes, and in a few moments we know that we have found and been found by another member of the Blessed Community. Sometimes we are thus suddenly knit together in the bonds of a love far faster than those of many years' acquaintance. In unbounded eagerness we seek for more such fellowship, and wonder at the apparent lethargy of mere 'members.'"[66]

Here's how Barbara Brown Taylor describes her kindred spirits, who seem very similar to mine: "I have learned to prize holy ignorance more highly than religious certainty and to seek

[64]Nikos Kazantzakis, *The Saviors of God: Spiritual Exercises* (New York: Simon and Schuster, 1960), 54.
[65]Thomas Kelly, *A Testament of Devotion* (New York: Harper and Row, 1941), 77–78.
[66]Kelly, 81.

companions who have arrived at the same place," she writes. "We are a motley crew, distinguished not only by our inability to explain ourselves to those who are more certain of their beliefs than we are, but in many cases by our distance from the centers of our faith communities as well."[67]

REVEAL YOURSELF IN YOUR CONGREGATION

If you're in a church, you may find surprising kindred spirits in your own congregation, as I did at midlife when for the first time my congregation received a pastor who in his sermons quoted from books he had read, and who unlike any previous pastor asked me about my interests. To help kindred spirits within the church find each other, it's important for pastors to reveal their own interests and concerns and ask members about theirs. Pastors can't merely assume they know all their members from what they see on the surface. And if you're a lay churchgoer who feels like a misfit, it's important for you to speak up in the church gatherings you attend. If kindred spirits are there, they probably think they're alone just as you think you are. Your speaking up will let you discover each other.

KEEP LOOKING

"Church shopping" has a bad name, especially among pastors, and understandably so. If you want to be part of the church, moving around without ever becoming part of any congregation probably isn't the best way. But the bad name, I suspect, comes partly from pastors' not wanting their church's attendance to drop and make them look bad. If you feel like a misfit in your present congregation, doing some church shopping can be helpful.

If in your shopping you find a congregation that looks the least bit encouraging, look deeper by visiting one or two of its

---

[67]Taylor, 224.

classes or projects. A church whose worship services turn you off may have a nonconformist Sunday School class like the one whose member told me it met in a dark corner of the basement, unknown to most other congregation members. To find your kindred spirits, be persistent, look for them in a variety of places, speak up about your concerns, and ask questions.

DON'T STAY QUIETLY OR LEAVE QUIETLY

What about leaving the church? For us misfits, it's hard to know whether staying or dropping out is the wisest thing to do. If we stay in a group that actively supports injustice or promotes beliefs we see as false, then by staying we're helping to perpetuate harmful practices that need to be stopped. But if we leave, we lose some opportunities to express our opposition and promote change.

"There may come a time when you have to leave the church to save your soul," says Joan Chittister, and I think she's right about that. (That's assuming that "save your soul" means "save your integrity," not "go to heaven when you die." I don't think going to church or staying away has any effect on what happens when we die.) And I think that what Chittister said next is equally important, maybe even more important. "But if you leave, don't leave quietly. And if you stay, don't stay quietly."[68]

Staying is sometimes the most faithful thing to do. However, if you stay in a congregation or denomination despite seeing it promoting injustice or spreading false information, be selective in which of its activities you support. Don't let your financial contributions or your visible presence help to perpetuate an unjust practice or reinforce a false interpretation of the Bible.

Also, speaking up about unfaithful practices you see happening in the church and why you're staying in spite of them is very important. Your speaking can help others see what's wrong too, and see the need to help remedy it. And if enough members see,

---

[68]Chittister, "Mysticism, Empowerment, and Resistance" seminar.

stay, and speak, they may be able to help that congregation or denomination become more like what God calls it to be. If everyone merely stays quietly, needed change isn't likely to happen.

In some circumstances, leaving can be the most faithful thing to do. If you're in a congregation in which many practices oppose the teaching and example of Jesus, you may need to leave, but you need to let members and outsiders know why you're leaving. Until enough people leave and make their reasons for leaving widely known, the congregation's unjust practices and presentations of misleading theology aren't likely to get changed.

START CLOSE TO HOME

Whether you're in a church or not, the first place to look for kindred spirits is probably in your local area. You may find some you don't expect. A woman whom Eric Elnes and his walkers met in a rural part of the United States—in a town that's actually named Podunk!—described a thriving, lifesaving group that met regularly in her home even though no one lived close to her and her area wasn't known for being open-minded. "There's this group we're part of that really keeps us sane," she told Elnes. "It gathers at our home each month to explore progressive faith and values. There's nearly twenty of us now. We read books together or watch videos and discuss them. In this group you can ask the kinds of questions and explore the kinds of issues that people are uncomfortable addressing in church. . . . It helps us feel connected and not so alone."[69]

When I read this I thought fondly of the similar group that meets at my home. I unexpectedly found some kindred spirits in my own area by starting a "Living the Questions" study course in my home a few years ago.[70] I was denied permission to do it in my

---

[69]Elnes, p. 95.

[70]For more information about this course and others offered by the same organization, see *www.livingthequestions.com* and the November 2007 issue of *Connections*, at *www.connectionsonline.org*.

church, so I sent a letter to everyone on my *Connections* mailing list who lived within about thirty miles of me, asking if any of them might be interested. To my surprise, more than twenty appeared. Several were people I knew, yet I hadn't previously known that they shared my church-related concerns. Some were members of my own congregation who had stopped attending because, like me, they felt like misfits in it and could not in good conscience support its present policies. The responders also included members of several other congregations and denominations, as well as some nonchurchgoers. Even though they all lived in the same relatively small geographical area, few of them knew each other.

The group is still going. A few from the original group have dropped out, but several new people have joined. It's a lifesaver for us. And I think we have attracted a more diverse group because of meeting in members' homes and being independent rather than being sponsored by a church, though of course many churches successfully sponsor similar studies.

Materials for courses of this type are more expensive than most individuals will be able or willing to invest in. Besides, few people have access to a mailing list as I do, and the cost of printing and postage for mailing an inquiry to a large list can be prohibitively expensive. So can the cost of a newspaper ad. But if you're determined, you may find a way to enlist such a group. A less expensive way could be to propose a study or discussion of a recent, thought-provoking book through your church or some other group you're in. Several of the books listed on my website include questions suitable for use in study groups, but suggested questions aren't essential. Readers of stimulating books usually come up with plenty of questions to talk about.

The first step for all potential group activities, however, even for a group of two, is making your concerns known in some way that lets you be recognized by kindred spirits who are nearby but have been keeping quiet because they thought they were alone.

CONVERSE BY E-MAIL, LOOK AT WEBSITES

If you can't find any kindred spirits to meet with regularly in person, for your own sanity and growth find some "spiritual friends" and stay in touch with them in other ways.

E-mail is an indispensable way for me. It may not be as satisfying as face-to-face conversation, but it's a lot better than nothing. Some of the kindred spirits I converse with by e-mail are people I know well and see occasionally. Others I've met in person but rarely see. Still others I know only by e-mail. I "met" most of those by their writing me about something they read in *Connections*. In most cases, neither they nor I have the time or desire to correspond regularly, but we recognize each other as kindred spirits and have e-mail conversations every now and then. And being reminded that they're out there helps keep me encouraged.

The internet also can be a way to find kindred spirits to communicate with, by e-mail or through their blogs or social-network sites if not in person. I'm mentioning some websites I'm aware of as I write this, but such things change, so by the time you read this, some of these addresses may not still lead to anything useful. So instead of depending on the sites I mention here, use a web search engine to look for groups and publications that identify themselves as "progressive."

The website of The Center for Progressive Christianity, *www.tcpc.org*, contains a big list of congregations, publications, and other Christian groups, projects, and materials that identify themselves as progressive. They're in many church denominations and some are unrelated to any denomination. This website may even help you find a congregation near you in which you can find kindred spirits. It also contains links to websites of other progressive groups.

The relatively new Progressive Christian Center of the South was started by a small group. Its website, *www.pccsouth.org*, has links to other progressive people and activities. It also includes articles about current issues as seen from a progressive Christian viewpoint.

If you're concerned about justice issues, look especially at websites of church-related groups with a social-justice focus. Several denominations include such groups. As a United Methodist, I'm most aware of the UMC's General Board of Church and Society, *www.umc-gbcs.org*, but other denominations have similar agencies. You also may find people who share your concerns by looking at the website of a political party or candidate whose aims are similar to yours. Look also for websites of authors whose books or articles you've liked.

ATTEND TALKS BY PROGRESSIVE CHRISTIANS

If you live in a relatively large city or can travel to one, you may find opportunities to attend events that are open to the public, at which progressive Christians speak. To find such events, consult city newspapers, radio, TV, or websites of progressive church-related groups. One that regularly presents such events featuring outstanding scholars, in various places around the United States, is the D. L. Dykes, Jr. Foundation, *www.faithandreason.org*. Attending events like these not only lets you hear thought-provoking content from the featured speakers. It also provides opportunities to meet kindred-spirit attenders.

Another way to hear top quality progressive speakers is by listening to them on CDs or DVDs. The Dykes Foundation offers many on its website. So does The Learning Company, *www.TEACH12.com*. You may also find such recordings at large bookstores, internet booksellers, and libraries.

FIND AUTHORS WHO GROAN IN YOUR LANGUAGE

For me, reading is an essential way of finding kindred spirits. A list of many of my favorite books is on my website, *www.connectionsonline.org*. I think of many authors as kindred spirits even though I've never seen them in person. Some are no longer living. So if you feel like a misfit and can't find kindred spirits to connect with in person, connect with some by reading their writing. "Hunt for writers who groan in your language," author Val Webb advises.[71]

I've made contact with several authors by writing to them. If a book doesn't include an address for its author, and he or she doesn't have a website with contact information, you can probably get a letter to him or her by sending it to the book's publisher and asking to have it forwarded to the author.

You may also find kindred-spirit authors by reading their articles in magazines that address current church-related topics from a forward-looking perspective. Two that I read regularly are *The Progressive Christian*, *www.tpcmagazine.org*, and *The Christian Century*, *www.christiancentury.org*. I suggest that you consider these and also look for others on the internet, in bookstores, or in a public library or the library of a university or seminary near you.

I used to think that all published authors were so busy and so much more accomplished than I that they wouldn't want to be bothered by getting mail from a nobody like me, but I've found that few are like that. Authors of best-sellers may be too busy to respond, but even with them, sending a question or note of thanks about their writing is worth a try. I've found that authors of less-than-best-selling books, even if they're fairly well known, tend to be delighted to hear from someone who has read their writing, thought carefully about it, and cared enough to respond.

As a writer, I experience this regularly. Readers of *Connections* often write me, and I greatly appreciate their comments and reply to most of them. Also, when a newspaper or magazine has occasionally had an article about *Connections* and mentioned some of my views, I've always gotten notes and calls from people who were surprised and delighted to find someone whose views were similar to theirs. Sometimes I've gotten together with one of these responders in person and enjoyed finding a new kindred-spirit friend.

---

[71]Val Webb, *In Defense of Doubt: An Invitation to Adventure* (St. Louis: Chalice Press, 1995), 127.

NETWORK, NETWORK, NETWORK

Waiting passively for kindred spirits to find you isn't likely to help you locate many. To find kindred spirits and promote the beliefs and issues you feel strongly about, especially if they're minority views within your church or your local area, it's essential to take the initiative and network, network, network. That doesn't come easily to me. As an introvert I'm rarely comfortable striking up conversations with people I don't know. But one of my helpful discoveries of the last several years is that I can do it and it's definitely worth doing. It can lead to interesting people and opportunities. One kindred spirit often leads to another. So if you feel like a church misfit and want to find kindred spirits, follow up on every possible clue.

PRAY IN MANY WAYS

At first I'm inclined to say that in addition to all these ways I've mentioned for finding kindred spirits—reading, talking with people, thinking, writing, hearing speakers, and so on—it's important to remember prayer as a way of finding new insights and kindred spirits. But all these activities I've mentioned *are* prayer. Prayer simply means trying to communicate with the divine in some way, and what that way is for any particular person depends on how he or she typically functions and on how he or she sees the divine.

From going to church and from hearing Christians talk, it's easy to get the impression that praying requires using certain words, being in a particular physical position, being in a special place, or addressing God in a particular way, but that impression is misleading. Those forms of prayer we hear most about may be valuable for some people, but they're not for everyone. They're not essential for anyone, and they're actually a hindrance to some.

One of my main ways of praying is writing. Writing *Connections* is part of that, but so is personal journaling—dumping thoughts, feelings, and questions into my computer or onto whatever paper happens to be available. I find journaling especially helpful for trying to sort out problems that I don't want to reveal to anyone but myself and God. The very act of putting them into words often helps me see things about them that I hadn't seen when they were only vague thoughts or feelings. Writing lets me get them out of my head, clarified, and into a form where I can acknowledge them and maybe even see something helpful to do about them. So although journaling isn't a way to find kindred spirits by directly contacting them, it can bring helpful new insights about ways of looking for them.

FIND YOUR "WOMB ROOM"

I've appreciated some other ways in which contemporary authors describe prayer. Filmmaker Stephen Vittoria believes, as I also do, that all forms of communication can be prayer if the person praying desires change that corrects injustice, sets people free, or heals hate with love or fear with compassion. He describes unselfish prayer as a revolutionary act demanding change.[72]

Rick Diamond calls prayer "the means by which, when we are willing to enter spirit space, we hear what the Spirit is doing, breathing, singing, saying, being." He assures us that "something we mumble in church or before we eat isn't what I'm talking about. Something the preacher says before a session of Congress isn't it either. Prayer is not knowing—and just going into that place."[73]

"That place" that Diamond refers to doesn't have to be any special "religious" place such as a church building. But many of us find that in certain physical places we're more likely to become aware of God than in other places. I love the name I once heard a woman give for that place in her experience: her "womb room."

---

[72]Malcolm Boyd and J. Jon Bruno, eds., *In Times Like These: How We Pray* (New York: Seabury/Church Publishing, Inc., 2005), 76.
[73]Diamond, 116.

It's the kind of place Matthew 6:6 refers to: "Whenever you pray, go into your room ['closet,' in the King James Version] and shut the door and pray to your Father who is in secret." It's the place where one's insights—which could be seen as answers to prayer—are most often conceived.

Mine is the shower. Maybe that's because its warmth, solitude, wetness, and closed-in feeling have something in common with the physical conditions inside a womb. Or maybe not. But for whatever reason, the shower often is where new insights or brainstorms strike me. The only problem with it is that I sometimes have a hard time hanging onto the thoughts that occur to me there, in the exact words I want to express them in, until I can get out and dry off and write them down. I often wish for a waterproof computer or at least a waterproof notepad for jotting them down in the shower before I lose my mental grip on them!

EXPOSE AND OPPOSE UNJUST GROUPS, AND SUPPORT MISTREATED MISFITS

Besides getting in touch with like-minded people, exposing and actively opposing groups and individuals that promote closed-minded, exclusivist, literalist, backward-looking views of the Bible and Christianity is vitally important for Christians. One such group that is especially well-funded and well-organized, thus very influential, is the Institute for Religion and Democracy. Like many other such groups, it has a name that sounds like it promotes good things. But it doesn't. It fiercely attacks the social-justice efforts of several mainline Protestant denominations. Organizations with similar harmful goals, which oppose many social-justice efforts of the United Methodist Church, are Good News and The Confessing Movement. Other church denominations include similar groups. If you're in a church, I urge you to become aware and help make other church members aware of such groups and the harmful views they promote. Many directly oppose major aspects of what Jesus taught and demonstrated.

Along with locating kindred spirits and opposing harmful views and practices, it's vital for all of us misfits also to support fellow misfits who are being attacked. These include pastors whose fearful, backward-looking members are trying to oust them because their views don't conform to all of those members' beliefs. Other misfits who need support may include lay church members who are being ignored or shunned because of what they're saying.

Fellow misfits may feel the greatest concern for these mistreated misfits, but fits also need to come to their rescue. It's fits, in fact, whose support is especially needed, because the fits are likely to be more numerous than misfits and to be in positions of greater institutional power. When I think of the need for fits to oppose the mistreatment of misfits, I think of a saying whose source seems to be unknown: "I may disagree with what you say, but I will defend to the death your right to say it." I wish more members actively followed that policy in the church.

KEEP LOOKING, KEEP THINKING

If you feel like a misfit in the church or feel spiritually homeless, I hope you'll try the ways I've mentioned here, to look for kindred spirits and community.

Whether you're a misfit or a fit, however, I hope you'll keep thinking about what you believe. Even more important, I hope you'll keep thinking about what behavior is resulting from your present beliefs and the beliefs you see others claiming.

That leads to thinking about what kind of behavior would be most helpful for our world, and thus what the purpose of the church is. That's the question that started me on the long journey I've been describing in this book. It's a question I'm still considering.

IX

Hope for Misfits and the Church

YEARS AGO, GETTING ANGRY about what was happening in my church congregation motivated me to look for what the church's purpose really was. I've learned a lot since then, but I'm still looking. I've come to the conclusion that none of us should ever stop looking. We all need to get informed and stay informed about many views and to keep thinking and talking about them.

I was recently reminded of something I read years ago in one of the books I accumulated when I browsed in bookstores—the books that apparently weren't read by anybody else I knew. One of those books mentioned the "theological conversation" within the church. When I read that, I realized "That's the aspect of the church I wish I could be part of!" But I knew that could never happen. At that time, my only church involvement was doing the expected women's background volunteer things in my local church. And even in it, I wasn't part of any planning or decision-making or even discussing. Only men did those things in my local church then, and I wasn't aware that even they ever talked about theology. I assumed that the theological conversation was carried on only by the men who were famous authors and professors or maybe bishops. Whoever they were, I knew they were very far, geographically and otherwise, from where I was and from the kinds of things that filled my day-to-day life.

Unbelievable as it would have seemed to me then, however, I now have at least a small voice in the theological conversation. Sometimes I converse one-to-one with some of those formerly remote-seeming people—authors, scholars, bishops, and other such people. But I also converse with many other churchgoers and church alumni/ae through *Connections* and now through this book.

If you're not already in the theological conversation in some way, I urge you to get into it. That's not impossible. The conversation needs to be happening openly and constantly in every local congregation and community, then moving up from there to the top of the church hierarchy. It needs to keep moving downward, too, by having the findings of scholars and the views of top church leaders disseminated openly and regularly in local congregations. If the conversation is not yet happening in your church or your community, then it's time for you to start it happening.

Today's widespread access to communication through the internet and other electronic methods makes participating in the theological conversation easier than it used to be. It's especially unfortunate, therefore, that so few church members seem interested in participating. Their lack of participation deprives the church and the world of sorely needed insights.

I want to stay in the conversation, so I'm still thinking and talking with others about what being a Christian really means. I'm sure it doesn't just mean what I assumed for the first forty or so years of my life—being baptized, going to church regularly, believing everything in the Bible, being nice, being a good citizen, and forcing oneself to believe certain things about God and Jesus whether they seemed believable or not. Many Christians evidently still see that list as what being a Christian requires, and they apparently see the purpose of the church as trying to get more people to do those things, but I don't.

MORE THAN A SPIRITUAL JACUZZI

Many churchgoers apparently believe, too, that the church's purpose is to provide friends, comfort, and a feeling of security for its members. They want the church to be an unchanging refuge from change and from the stress of what happens outside the church walls. They want it to be for them what Benedictine sister Joan Chittister calls a spiritual Jacuzzi—a provider of warm, soothing escapism.[74] In my view, as apparently in hers, that's essentially the opposite of the church's purpose, yet many congregations make it seem to be their purpose.

A *Connections* reader's letter recently reminded me of that. "I do not have a church group," a prominent leader in his city and his profession wrote to me. He went on to say that he had participated in a church at a couple of times earlier in his life but had fallen away each time. He explained that he saw religious belief as a very personal part of a person's belief system, implying that being in a church group wasn't necessary for it. He continued, "Most of my church attendance in recent years has been at funerals, where a church can provide great comfort. A major attraction of church affiliation is the fellowship and comfort that goes with active participation."

The rest of this man's letter made clear that what he hadn't seen churches providing was food for thought. He reads widely and thinks deeply, and he has obviously thought seriously about what he believes. But he hasn't seen churches promoting or even welcoming such things. It's no wonder that he doesn't have any interest in being part of a church just to get friends and comfort, which he already gets plenty of in other ways. And unfortunately, far too many churches present the same misleading picture that he has gotten: that religious belief is only personal, and that providing fellowship and comfort is all that churches are for.

---

[74]Joan Chittister, "Mysticism, Empowerment, & Resistance" seminar.

Religious belief is in one sense personal, but true Christian faith goes far beyond that. It is about changing the world, and when churches don't motivate their members to work toward that, those churches seem to me to be ignoring the church's main purpose. Fellowship and comfort are enjoyable, but to both church members and outsiders, the church needs to make apparent that fellowship and comfort are nowhere near the main things it exists to provide.

FRIENDSHIP—THE MAIN THING OR AN INCIDENTAL?

Friendship is a powerful tie to the church even for many people who feel like misfits with regard to other aspects of the church. Many who are very turned off by what they see as major church shortcomings don't find those reason enough to leave. They want to stay with church friends, no matter what else is happening in the church.

In fact, being with friends seems to be the main motivation of most churchgoers whether they're fits or misfits. It definitely seems to take precedence over beliefs. It takes precedence, too, over concern about injustice in society and about church shortcomings, no matter how harmful these members recognize those to be. For many members, the church is a mainly place to find likable friends and enjoyable activities to take part in regularly with those friends. It's a place to feel known and wanted. It's a place to find people to feel close to in the midst of the impersonal, scary, and often dangerous surroundings we all live in. It's also a place to find people to rely on when disaster strikes—life-threatening illness, a loved one's death, the loss of a job, or a hurricane or tornado.

In these churchgoers' minds, the church isn't a group that gets together to carry out any kind of mission. It may be a place to find opportunities for helping those less fortunate and to feel good about doing that, but it isn't a group even remotely intended to change the world. It doesn't ask *why* some people are less fortunate than others, or try to lessen the causes of suffering.

Besides being a place for being with friends, for many churchgoers the church is a place for being reassured that their opinions, feelings, and beliefs are correct. It's a place for these churchgoers to be reassured that they're okay and that they'll still be okay after they die.

We might all like to have these benefits, but is furnishing them the church's purpose? I don't think so. Some may be welcome extras but not the main purpose, while others actually seem contrary to the church's purpose. But whether we see them as essentials, extras, or mistakes, "What's the real purpose of the church?" is a question we all need to ask and keep asking.

IS THE WILL OF THE MAJORITY GOD'S WILL?

The basic purpose of the church, whatever we discern it to be, needs to drive all that we do in the institutional church. But what if we don't all agree on what the purpose is?

Many church members seem to think that the views of the majority of members should determine what the church does. But throughout history, what Christians have eventually come to see as God's will has often been the opposite of the will of the majority. And yet, as a practical matter, how can we make reasonable decisions in any group, including the church, other than by majority vote or consensus? Is our only hope that, if a minority voice is speaking for God, it will change the majority's opinion eventually? I wish we'd at least acknowledge such questions as important in the church, when we think about our purpose and how to carry it out.

MAKING OR ATTRACTING?

My denomination's official purpose is "to make disciples of Jesus Christ for the transformation of the world," and other denominations express their purpose in similar ways. But that way of describing Christianity's purpose doesn't seem quite right to me. What seems to me much more desirable and also more likely to be effective is to try to *attract* people by showing them that transformation of the world is needed and that through the church they could help accomplish it. To me, *attracting* people in that way is far preferable to trying to *make* them into anything. There's something manipulative and arrogant about wanting to *make* people into followers of our particular beliefs.

Also, I'd rather try to attract people not necessarily to Jesus himself but rather to behaving in the way that he taught and demonstrated, whatever name we may give it. Too often, trying to persuade people to become disciples of Jesus means trying to get them to believe a particular set of doctrines and to believe that only Christianity has the truth, which like many other misfits I find impossible to believe.

So although it wouldn't be as concise a statement for church publicity purposes, I'd much prefer our saying that our purpose is to show people how following the way that Jesus taught can transform the world in beneficial ways. Author Madeleine L'Engle expressed something similar by saying, "We do not convince others by loudly discrediting what they believe, by telling them how wrong they are and how right we are. We convince them by showing them a light that is so lovely that they will want with all their hearts to know the source of it."[75]

RELIGIONS' PURPOSE AND CHRISTIANITY'S PURPOSE

As I've kept thinking about all this, I've come to see my search as involving several related questions. I started with the particular question of what the purpose of the church was. That led me to investigate what the purpose of Christianity was.

I still see that question as important. I believe that answering it is important not only for everyone who is part of the church but also for everyone who lives in a country in which the majority

---

[75]Madeleine L'Engle, *Walking on Water* (New York: Bantam Books, 1980), 122.

of citizens are at least nominally Christian. The answer is even important for everyone else in the world, because so many of the world's people are nominally Christian. If Christianity's purpose is to make everyone into Christians, as many Christians believe it is, then non-Christians need to know that, because it makes them targets of Christians' efforts to convert them. But if Christianity's purpose is instead to make life better for more people by practicing love and justice, as I believe it is, then non-Christians have no reason to see Christians as a threat. In fact, some non-Christians might even want to join the Christians in trying to carry out that purpose, whether or not they did it under the Christian label.

Thinking about the purpose of the church and thus of Christianity has therefore led me to think also about the larger question of the purpose of all religion.

INSIGHTS FROM THE WORLD'S RELIGIONS

In her book *The Great Transformation*, scholar and former Roman Catholic nun Karen Armstrong describes what all of the world's major religions originally saw as their purpose. She writes about the time that has come to be called the Axial Age, the period from about 900 to 200 BCE. This is the period, Armstrong explains, during which "the great world traditions that have continued to nourish humanity came into being: Confucianism and Daoism in China; Hinduism and Buddhism in India; monotheism in Israel; and philosophical rationalism in Greece." Both Christianity and Islam arose as religions after the Axial Age, but their roots were in it. Armstrong sees the following insights as having emerged from the major religions during that period.

- No statement about the divine can fully define it.

- The appropriate attitude toward the sacred is reverent silence.

- What matters most is how one behaves, not what one claims to believe.

- Questioning beliefs and testing them against experience is essential.

- Examining one's own behavior is more important than lambasting others' behavior. Beliefs that make one belligerent, intolerant, and cruel are not sound.

- Being moral means being compassionate, not just to one's own people but also to the stranger.

- Being compassionate and rejecting aggression is the route to the divine and to profound personal change.[76]

I'm not sure that silence is the only appropriate response to the divine, although it's my most natural response. But in my view, all the others of these insights mentioned by Armstrong are consistent with the church's true purpose and need more emphasis by churches. In fact, her list comes very close to describing my present religious beliefs.

RELIGION'S PURPOSE?

As I've considered views of many thinkers, inside and outside of the church, I've come to the tentative conclusion that religion at its best serves three valuable purposes.

- To help people become aware of the sacred and discern how it seems to operate. That means helping them recognize how divine activity or presence appears in our world. It includes asking what the divine is like: Does it exist? If so, is it a person-like being? If not, what? Does it control all that happens? Can we influence it in any way? If so, how?

- To help people get in sync with the way in which the sacred operates. That means living in ways that enhance its operation,

---

[76]Armstrong, *The Great Transformation*.

if that's possible, but at least in ways that cooperate with it rather than ignore or try to oppose it. These might include protecting the natural environment, not building in flood plains, and eating healthy foods.

- To make human life better. Many religious beliefs and practices are mainly efforts to ensure the personal survival and comfort of adherents and their loved ones, by doing what they think will bring divine favor and avoid divine wrath. At its best, however, religion can promote efforts to make life better for all, through building community, promoting peace, protecting the natural world, and treating all people with compassion and justice.

THE QUESTION FOR CHRISTIANS

Christianity has its particular ways of aiming at these three purposes, just as other religions have theirs. The question for the church is how to work toward these purposes in ways consistent with the teachings of Jesus. That means focusing on what he apparently gave top priority to, and avoiding and opposing behavior that differs from what he taught and demonstrated.

Having this focus often means acting differently from the people around us, even if they are our friends, family, or fellow church members. That means being a nonconformist—a misfit—in some ways. It means taking personal responsibility and initiative for helping to bring about needed change. It means refusing to be an enabler of church practices and government policies that prevent the compassion and justice Jesus practiced and taught. That means refusing to perpetuate such policies and practices by continuing to participate in them or by keeping quiet when we see them being practiced. It means staying open to new information and new insight—in fact, deliberately searching for new information and insight—and then revising our beliefs and behavior whenever we feel that they're not consistent with what we've discovered.

FOLLOWING JESUS MEANS BEING A MISFIT

Working toward these purposes and acting on these insights often results in feeling like a misfit and being seen as a misfit by others. That can be very uncomfortable. It's risky, too. It can result in being attacked, even by fellow church members. But if we're serious about following Jesus, neither comfort, popularity, nor even personal safety can be our main goals.

If we want to follow Jesus, we'll have to follow the advice the apostle Paul gave in his letter to the church at Rome:

> Do not be conformed to this world, but be transformed by the renewing of your minds, so that you may discern what is the will of God (Romans 12:2).

Following that advice requires getting involved. It requires being active instead of passive. It includes not conforming to the institutional church when we see it straying from what Jesus emphasized most. It means we must push for change when we see the church treating people cruelly, cooperating with empire instead of opposing it, or aiming at merely keeping members comfortable instead of promoting justice.

THE FAITHFULNESS OF ASKING QUESTIONS

Renewing your mind, as Paul advises, means changing your way of thinking. That requires asking questions and continuing to ask questions. It means never deluding yourself into thinking you've found all the answers.

I like what Sister Joan Chittister says about the importance of doing that.

> I heard of a woman who, finding herself drifting toward the middle of a dangerously feminist conversation, stopped the group in the midst of the process. "I don't want to hear any more about any of this," she said, "because if I did, I would have to change my life." A wise woman. It is always so much easier to assuage pain than to cure it, so much easier to accept a thing than to question it.

The ability—the commitment—to question, to examine every aspect of the human journey is the only form of fidelity worth the price of admission to this sojourn called life. . . . It is the questions we ask that move us from stage to stage of growing, that take us from level to level of our thoughts, however simple the questions may seem. . . .

"Everything that deceives," Plato said, "can be said to enchant." I have been enchanted by far too many falsehoods in life. I would rather go on living the struggle than go comatose in the face of answers that are not true, were never true, cannot possibly be true. Most of all, I have indeed found that the process of examining them has made my life worthwhile.[77]

In the church, I often see untruthful answers being presented as if they were truths. I also see many people who seem to have gone comatose in the face of those answers. Even worse, I see many who seem determined to remain comatose. Worst of all, instead of helping to bring comatose people out of their comas, I see the church actively helping them to stay comatose or even to die spiritually.

> *I came that they may have life, and have it abundantly.*
> —JOHN 10:10

That's spiritual euthanasia, and it's especially disturbing to see happening in an institution that claims to be following one who said he came to bring life. I believe all of us who care about the well-being of the church and the world need to make our best efforts to combat that deadly way of functioning. This book is part of my effort.

---

[77]Joan Chittister, "Afterword: The Power of Questions to Propel: A Retrospective," in Mary Hembrow Snyder, ed., *Spiritual Questions for the Twenty-First Century: Essays in Honor of Joan D. Chittister* (Maryknoll, NY: Orbis Books, 2001), 167–187.

HOPE FOR THE CHURCH

Increasing numbers of other Christians are also making efforts. As a result, many observers see hope for the church even though they feel sure that it won't continue in exactly the form longtime churchgoers have been used to.

Eric Elnes is one of those hopeful observers. The picture he got from walking across America, he says, was quite different from what is portrayed in the media or by popular religious leaders. The picture, he writes, is "both surprising and encouraging for those of us who have been critical of the excesses of Christian fundamentalism and the sterility of liberalism. The picture . . . is of no less than the emergence of a new form of Christian faith at the grass roots that transcends traditional labels and stereotypes. This faith is more concerned with honesty than morality, more with embracing differences than with judging others, and more with pushing boundaries than with creating them."[78]

One of the pastors Elnes met during his walk was similarly hopeful. "The way I see it," she observed, "the institution of the church may be dying, but the church is more alive now than ever. The true church is made up of people led by the Spirit. The church is being brought to life in our time. Collapse is actually waking the church up."[79]

Theologian Val Webb is hopeful, too. She believes "a new Christianity is evolving, uncovering the human Jesus so long buried under centuries of dogma."[80]

Canadian pastor Gretta Vosper sees hope despite seeing chaos. "Chaos has erupted in the mainline church," she observes, and she assures us that some of the needed change won't be easy or comfortable. "Broad-vision change," she explains, "is not 'new-curtains' window-dressing change but real, deep down, 'this is going to hurt' change. It can be liberating and refreshing, but it

---

[78]Elnes, ix.
[79]Elnes, 98.
[80]Webb, *Like Catching Water in a Net*, 206.

comes with costs." Still, Vosper sees a bright side. "In moments of utter chaos, great things can happen. The dissolution of order allows for new patterns to emerge, new relationships to form."[81]

Phyllis Tickle, a lay minister in the Episcopal Church and founding editor of the religion department of *Publishers Weekly*, bases her hope on the fact that what she calls "holy rummage sales" have happened about every five hundred years throughout Christian history and no standing form of organized Christian faith has ever been destroyed by one of these eruptions. "When an overly institutionalized form of Christianity is, or ever has been, battered into pieces and opened to the air of the world around it," Tickle observes, "that faith-form has both itself spread and also enabled the spread of the young upstart that afflicted it."[82]

All of us who are hopeful about the church's future see that turning our hopes into reality will require some changes, so we're speaking out about the need for change. Our churches may see us as misfits, even as heretics who need to be shunned or ousted. But if we care about helping to make the world more loving, peaceful, and just, we can't let that deter us. We need to be cheerleaders for the church when we honestly can, but to be persistent, vocal critics when we see the church failing to follow the teaching of Jesus.

A PRAYER FOR FITS AND MISFITS

Thank you for considering the views I've expressed here. As I leave them with you I offer the prayer known as "A Franciscan Benediction." I offer it for you, for myself, and for the many other misfits and fits who want to help the church and the world become more loving and more just, and who in doing that want to find real community.

---

[81]Gretta Vosper, *With or Without God: Why the Way We Live Is More Important Than What We Believe* (Toronto: Harper Perennial, 2008), 2, 5.

[82]Phyllis Tickle, *The Great Emergence: How Christianity Is Changing and Why* (Grand Rapids, MI: Baker Books, 2008), 28.

May God bless you with discomfort
At easy answers, half-truths, and superficial relationships,
So that you may live deep within your heart.

May God bless you with anger
At injustice, oppression, and exploitation of people,
So that you may work for justice, freedom, and peace.

May God bless you with tears
To shed for those who suffer from pain, rejection, starvation,
    and war,
So that you may reach out your hand to comfort them
And to turn their pain into joy.

And may God bless you with enough foolishness
To believe that you can make a difference in this world,
So that you can do what others claim cannot be done. Amen.[83]

---

[83]Source unknown.

Appendix A

Questions to Think or Talk About

INTRODUCTION: HEARING MISFITS' CRIES

When you attend church activities or hear Christians talk, do you feel like a fit or a misfit?

If you're a fit, how do you think your church should deal with its misfits?

If you're a misfit who attends a church, how do you deal with having views that the majority of members disagree with?

If you've left the church or never been active in a church, do you have a community of kindred spirits to be part of, to talk about beliefs and pursue humanitarian projects?

CHAPTER I—KEEPING QUIET, TRYING TO FIT

Have you ever thought back through as much of your life story as Barbara tells of hers here?

Have you ever shared your story and your feelings about it with anyone? If so, how did he or she react?

If you grew up attending a church, what do you remember about it? How did you feel about it?

Have your views about gender roles or about people of races or sexual orientations different from yours changed over the course of your life? If so, how?

Have you ever felt the pain of staying in a tight bud, and felt the urge to blossom? If so, what did you do about it?

CHAPTER II—WAKING UP, SPEAKING OUT

Has a change in your life ever motivated you to reevaluate your beliefs, as church turmoil did for Barbara?

Have you ever felt the need to change your way of relating to your parents or your grown children? If so, did you make the change? What was the result?

Have you ever made a change as big as any of those Barbara made at midlife? If so, how do you feel now about having made it?

Has your spiritual journey included points at which you started moving in a new direction? If so, what triggered the change? What obstacles did you experience?

What change might you need to make now?

CHAPTER III—MANY MISFITS WITH THE SAME MESSAGES

Do you identify with what Barbara keeps hearing from *Connections* readers?

If so, how have you dealt with such features of the church that you find disturbing? If not, how do you feel your church should deal with people who have such concerns?

Should the views of the majority determine what the church does? How can we deliberately take minority views into account?

If Jesus came to your church, how do you think he would react to what he observed there? How do you think he would be treated?

Does your church have members who provide a "ministry of irritation" or express "holy discontent"? How do you think the church should deal with such members?

CHAPTER IV—ALL DIFFERENT, ALL NEEDED

How important to you are the words of hymns, anthems, prayers, and other parts of typical worship services?

How do you feel about what Barbara sees as the three main areas in which fits and misfits differ? How should the church deal with these differences?

Can you identify with some of the personality traits that Barbara describes? One of the stages of faith? Do you find such methods of categorizing helpful?

CHAPTER V—WHAT CONGREGATIONS CAN DO

How do you feel about the need to discuss controversial issues in the church? About the need to hear minority views?

If you're in a church or have been in one, have you ever been asked to share all or part of your story in any church group? Have you heard others share theirs? Would/Did you find sharing stories welcome? scary? interesting? worthwhile?

If you're a pastor, how do you let misfits know they are welcome?

Have you ever kept quiet about your views or questions because you didn't hear anyone else saying anything similar? Why?

In your church or city or the wider world, are there any people who you think may be speaking for God? How are they being treated?

How should the church determine how much diversity in beliefs it will permit members to express within the church?

What are the essentials for being Christian?

CHAPTER VI—WHAT MISFITS WANT TO KNOW

If you're a pastor, do you regularly reveal what you know about the origin and development of the Bible, or the origin of doctrines and creeds, in worship services? Do you reveal your personal questions and doubts, or your real beliefs, even if they differ from your denomination's official positions or from what the majority of your members believe?

How might your congregation change its worship or decision-making bodies to make misfits feel welcome?

How would you feel about using varied translations of the Lord's Prayer in worship services?

What new activities might your church need to offer in order to make misfits feel welcome?

How can the church make misfits feel welcome without driving off the fits?

CHAPTER VII—WHAT THE CHURCH AND THE WORLD NEED TO KNOW

Did any of the information about the Bible, Jesus, or doctrines in this chapter come as a surprise to you? If so, how did you feel about becoming aware of it? Would you like to hear more such information from the church?

Should Christians oppose empire as it appears in today's world? How do you feel about America being called today's Rome?

Is the church right to put more emphasis on personal salvation than on liberation and social justice, unlike where Jesus apparently put his main emphasis?

Should the church present concepts like the Trinity and substitutionary atonement as if they were facts and were essential Christian beliefs?

Do you see ancient church councils' statements as more likely to represent truth than the official statements of today's church decision-making bodies?

CHAPTER VIII—WHAT MISFITS CAN DO

Do you have kindred spirits with whom to think, talk, and worship?

Have you had some friends recede in significance and others "step forward in your attention," as Thomas Kelly describes? If so, what caused the change? How did you feel about it?

Do you have a "womb room"—a place where you most often find new insights emerging?

Are there certain places or circumstances in which you feel closest to God?

CHAPTER IX—HOPE FOR MISFITS AND THE CHURCH

Are you taking part in the church's theological conversation?

What do you think being a Christian requires?

What do you see as the purpose of the church?

What do you see as the purpose of religion?

Appendix B

Credo

RELIGIONS

I see the basic aim of all religions as discovering how the divine (the sacred, the holy) operates, mainly in the hope of influencing it. Religions' adherents try to obtain divine favor and avoid divine wrath by doing what they see as the will of the divine and by praying. Their aim is to keep themselves and their loved ones alive and supplied with life's necessities and to increase their comfort and happiness.

GOD

Christians call the divine "God" and refer to how God operates as God's will or nature. Most Christians see the Bible and the doctrine of the Trinity as the main sources of information about God. Many see these as the only valid sources. However, the Bible presents only the experiences and beliefs of one particular cultural and historical group, as reported through a complex centuries-long process of oral storytelling and then writing, selecting, compiling, copying, translating, and editing. And the doctrine of the Trinity is merely how some leaders who lived several centuries after Jesus expressed their beliefs. In my view, therefore, neither of these sources can legitimately be seen as providing literal, accurate, or complete descriptions of what God is like, what God has done, or what God has communicated to human beings.

I find many of the Bible's portrayals of God unbelievable, but they are understandable because of how long ago the Bible's contents originated. What is not understandable to me is that the institutional church and so many individual Christians still portray God only as the Bible does, as being in the sky above us in a flat, three-level world. The church also portrays God in many ways that even contradict what it claims to believe God is like. It says God is spirit, yet it constantly portrays God as a person-like being. It says God is timeless, but it often speaks to and about God in 17th-century English. It says God has no gender, but it portrays God almost exclusively as male. The church often portrays God specifically as a Santa-Claus-like man who capriciously, unpredictably, and unexplainably gives some people what they ask for but denies the requests of others. Many Christians portray God as an all-powerful being who allows or even causes disasters such as tornados, wrecks, and illnesses to kill some people while saving others from the same disasters. These portrayals contradict much of today's best thinking. But many people are incorrectly labeled atheists merely because they do not find these particular descriptions of God believable.

A BEING? AN ORDER? IMPOSSIBLE TO KNOW

I understand the divine not as a being but rather as something like the order, pattern, or system of principles underlying all aspects of the cosmos (that is, of total reality, whatever that may include). Knowing exactly what this infinite pattern or system is like or how it functions is surely impossible for finite human beings. However, I can't believe that it deals individually or personally with people. It may be loving in the sense of operating beneficially for the overall system or for whoever and whatever acts in accord with its principles rather than against them. But I believe the divine is neutral in that it does not deliberately do good or bad for particular individuals or groups in response to their personal needs, behavior, beliefs, or requests.

JESUS—CHRISTIANITY'S MODEL

I believe compassion (love), nonviolence, and justice are the goals of Christianity because it arose from the life of Jesus and is based on following his example, and he apparently practiced and taught these behaviors. I believe that sin consists of being uncompassionate, violent, or unjust—harming people or other parts of the natural world. I believe that practices that do not harm others (mutually chosen sexual practices, for example) are not sinful.

Justice as seen by true Christianity is not merely punishing criminals. Instead, it is helping all people to have enough of life's necessities. It is treating no human beings as inferior because of their race, sex, class, or other such characteristics. Christians' source of authority for this meaning of justice is partly the prophetic tradition described in what we call the Old Testament, but it is mainly the Bible's descriptions of Jesus.

However, practicing compassion, nonviolence, and justice is important not merely because Jesus advocated it but rather because it seems likely to make life better for the most people. If those practices result from being an adherent of Islam, Hinduism, any other religion, or of no formal religion, then following that religion is as worthwhile as being a Christian. And if an individual or group fails to practice and promote compassion, nonviolence, and justice, then that individual or group's religion is worth little. In fact, it can be harmful, even if it bears the name "church" or "Christian."

Because of how the Bible originated and developed, I don't believe that everything it says about Jesus can legitimately be considered historical or that all the sayings it attributes to him can be considered verbatim quotes. I don't believe we know exactly what Jesus said or did. Still, we can probably get a relatively accurate picture of him by analyzing the Bible's contents along with other documents and artifacts from the setting in which he lived, plus the views of scholars. Being aware of such findings and opinions is therefore important.

NO SPECIAL ACCESS TO GOD OR HEAVEN

I don't believe Jesus was divine in any unique way, although he may have somehow been more fully in touch with the divine and more able to communicate it than most other human beings are. This characteristic apparently is what has led many followers to feel, during his earthly life and succeeding centuries, that through him they experience the divine. This characteristic has also inspired many followers to create magnificent artistic and intellectual works and to do valuable service to humanity. But I do not believe Jesus is still alive in any supernatural way.

Neither do I believe that imitating Jesus or declaring belief in him gives special access to God or assurance of "going to heaven" at death. I believe that following his teaching and example can help improve earthly life, but I can't believe that it determines what will happen in any afterlife. I see "heaven" and "hell" as merely names for what people would like to have or to avoid after death.

PROMOTING AWARENESS

Furthering the kind of compassion, peace, and justice demonstrated by Jesus—what his earliest followers called "The Way"—requires the church to make not only its members but also the general public aware of what has now become known about the earthly life of Jesus, the Roman Empire setting in which he lived, and the ways in which he actively opposed its oppressive features. The church also needs to promote awareness of similarly oppressive features of today's world and of the need to expose and oppose them.

I believe that in order to present a realistic picture of Christianity, of Jesus, and of what following him today requires, the church also must actively promote awareness of how the Bible originated and developed, how Christianity has developed and varied over the centuries, and how other religions' beliefs and sacred documents resemble some of Christianity's doctrines and the Bible's contents. Church members need to know that, like Christianity, other ancient religions worshiped dying and rising gods. Members need to know that many ancient people referred not only to their gods but also to prominent human leaders as sons of God, as having been born of virgins impregnated by gods, and as having ascended to heaven when they died. Such claims are not unique to Christianity and can't legitimately be interpreted literally.

SACRAMENTAL CHURCH PRACTICES

I believe that Christian practices such as baptism and Communion (Eucharist) may have psychological and spiritual value that comes from performing actions that symbolize cleansing, newness, and commitment to love and justice. I believe that publicly expressing such commitment can strengthen it. But I don't believe that God initiated or commands these practices or that they affect whether or not one "goes to heaven" at death. Neither do I believe that only clergy can legitimately administer them or that their effect depends on using particular words, materials, or gestures.

NONCONFORMITY

I believe that following Jesus—being a Christian—often requires refusing to act "nice" and "sweet." It often requires being a nonconformist. It can require breaking some rules, or even some laws, and opposing some social customs. It requires critically evaluating what one's nation does. It can require refusing to support some government policies. Jesus apparently did that often.

Being Christian also requires critically evaluating the actions and policies of the institutional church. It can require refusing to participate in some of what the church does. Jesus did the equivalent of that, with regard to the established religion of his time and place.

CONNECTION TO GOD AND OTHERS

I suspect that some kind of nonphysical connection exists between people, between people and the divine, and maybe also with animals and even inanimate things, and that what Christians call "the Holy Spirit" refers to this connection. I believe that "spiritual practices" such as prayer can tap into it somehow. I believe that interaction with others often reveals the divine through this unseen connection.

I see being part of a community as valuable. But that community doesn't have to be the institutional church. I don't consider participating in the institutional church essential for Christians. Participation is misleading, in fact, when the church presents narrow portrayals of the divine and outdated, uninformed, literalist, unquestioned interpretations of the Bible and ancient creeds and doctrines. And when a church follows and promotes unjust and uncompassionate practices, as some churches do, participation in that church can even be harmful.

CONTINUAL REEVALUATION AND REVISION

I believe that maturing includes continually examining and revising one's beliefs to take new information and insight into account. Consequently, the beliefs I have expressed here are likely to change. And I believe that having perfectly complete or correct knowledge of God or anything else is impossible for humans, so some of these beliefs are undoubtedly mistaken.

Bibliography

Alter, Alexandra. "Banned from church." *The Wall Street Journal,* Jan. 18, 2008.

Armstrong, Karen. *The Great Transformation: The Beginnings of Our Religious Traditions.* New York: Alfred A. Knopf, 2006.

————. *The Case for God.* New York: Alfred A Knopf, 2009

Baldwin, George W. *A Political Reading of the Life of Jesus.* New York: iUniverse, 2006.

Bass, Diana Butler. *Christianity for the Rest of Us: How the Neighborhood Church Is Transforming the Faith.* New York: HarperSanFrancisco, 2006.

Borg, Marcus, and John Dominic Crossan. *The First Christmas: What the Gospels Really Say About Jesus's Birth.* New York: HarperCollins, 2007.

————. *The Last Week: A Day-by-Day Account of Jesus's Final Week in Jerusalem.* New York: HarperSanFrancisco, 2006.

Boyd, Malcolm, and J. Jon Bruno, eds. *In Times Like These: How We Pray.* New York: Seabury/Church Publishing, Inc., 2005.

Brueggemann, Walter. First Plenary Presentation of *The Prospect of a World Community of Religions: Domination or Collaboration?* Jackson, MS: D. L. Dykes, Jr. Foundation, Faith and Reason Symposium 2005 at Millsaps College.

Bruno, J. Jon, and Malcolm Boyd, eds. *In Times Like These: How We Pray.* New York: Seabury/Church Publishing, Inc., 2005.

Buechner, Frederick. *Telling Secrets: A Memoir.* New York: HarperSanFrancisco, 1991.

Chittister, Joan. "Afterword: The Power of Questions to Propel: A Retrospective," in Mary Hembrow Snyder, ed., *Spiritual Questions for the Twenty-First Century: Essays in Honor of Joan D. Chittister.* Maryknoll, NY: Orbis Books, 2001.

————. *In Search of Belief.* Liguori, MO: Liguori Publications, 2006.

————. "Mysticism, Empowerment, and Resistance" seminar presented by the D.L. Dykes, Jr. Foundation in Austin, Texas, May 18–20, 2006.

Crossan, John Dominic, and Marcus Borg. *The First Christmas: What the Gospels Really Say About Jesus's Birth.* New York: HarperCollins, 2007.

————. *The Last Week: A Day-by-Day Account of Jesus's Final Week in Jerusalem.* New York: HarperSanFrancisco, 2006.

Diamond, Rick. *Wrestling with God.* Lake Mary, FL: Relevant Books, 2003.

Dick, Dan R. *Vital Signs: A Pathway to Congregational Wholeness.* Nashville: Discipleship Resources, 2007.

Easterling, Larry W., and Barbara Wendland. *Spiritual Family Trees: Finding Your Faith Community's Roots.* Herndon, VA: The Alban Institute, 2001.

Elnes, Eric. *Asphalt Jesus: Finding a New Faith Along the Highways of America.* San Francisco: Wiley/Jossey-Bass, 2007.

Ferguson, Marilyn. *The Aquarian Conspiracy: Personal and Social Transformation in the 1980s.* Los Angeles: J. P. Tarcher, Inc., 1980.

Fletcher, Joseph. *Situation Ethics: The New Morality.* Louisville: Westminster John Knox Press, 1966.

Fowler, James W. *Stages of Faith: The Psychology of Human Development and the Quest for Meaning.* New York: HarperSanFrancisco, 1981/1995.

Good, Jack. *The Dishonest Church.* Scotts Valley, CA: Rising Star Press, 2003; reprinted by St. Johann Press, Haworth, NJ, 2008.

Harris, Sam. *Letter to a Christian Nation.* New York: Random House/Vintage Books, 2008.

————. *The End of Faith: Religion, Terror, and the Future of Reason.* New York: W. W. Norton & Co., 2004.

Hendricks, Obery M., Jr. *The Politics of Jesus: Rediscovering the True Revolutionary Nature of Jesus' Teachings and How They Have Been Corrupted*. New York: Doubleday/Three Leaves, 2006.

Herbert, T. Walter. *Faith-Based War: From 9/11 to Catastrophic Success in Iraq*. Oakville, CT: Equinox Press, 2009.

Holthaus, Gary. *The Unauthorized Bible: Selected Readings*. North Berwick, ME: BW Press, 2003.

Howe, Leroy. *Angry People in the Pews: Managing Anger in the Church*. Valley Forge, PA: Judson Press, 2001.

Kazantzakis, Nikos. *The Saviors of God: Spiritual Exercises*. New York: Simon and Schuster, 1960.

Kelly, Thomas. *A Testament of Devotion*. New York: Harper and Row, 1941.

Killen, Patricia O'Connell. *Finding Our Voices: Women, Wisdom, and Faith*. New York: Crossroad Publishing Co., 1997.

Larson, Bruce, and Keith Miller. *The Edge of Adventure: An Experiment in Faith*. Waco, TX: Word Books, 1974.

L'Engle, Madeleine. *Walking on Water*. New York: Bantam Books, 1980.

Levine, Amy-Jill. *The Misunderstood Jew: The Church and the Scandal of the Jewish Jesus*. New York: HarperSanFrancisco, 2006.

Meyers, Robin. *Saving Jesus from the Church: How To Stop Worshiping Christ and Start Following Jesus*. New York: HarperCollins, 2009.

Miller, Keith, and Bruce Larson. *The Edge of Adventure: An Experiment in Faith*. Waco, TX: Word Books, 1974.

Ricker, George M. *What You Don't Have To Believe To Be a Christian*. Austin, TX: Sunbelt Eakin, 2002.

Rieger, Joerg. *Christ and Empire: From Paul to Postcolonial Times*. Minneapolis: Fortress Press, 2007.

Rohr, Richard. *Hope Against Darkness: The Transforming Vision of Saint Francis in an Age of Anxiety*. Cincinnati: St Anthony Messenger Press, 2001.

Sataline, Susan. "A Popular Strategy for Church Growth Splits Congregants Across the United States." *The Wall Street Journal*, Sept. 5, 2006.

Spong, John Shelby. *The Sins of Scripture: Exposing the Bible's Texts of Hate to Reveal the God of Love.* New York: HarperSanFrancisco, 2005.

Taylor, Barbara Brown. *Leaving Church: A Memoir of Faith.* New York: HarperSanFrancisco, 2006.

Teilhard de Chardin, Pierre. *The Divine Milieu.* New York: Harper & Row, 1960.

Tickle, Phyllis. *The Great Emergence: How Christianity Is Changing and Why.* Grand Rapids, MI: Baker Books, 2008.

Vosper, Gretta. *With or Without God: Why the Way We Live Is More Important Than What We Believe.* Toronto: Harper Perennial, 2008.

Webb, Val. *In Defense of Doubt: An Invitation to Adventure.* St. Louis: Chalice Press, 1995.

————. *Like Catching Water in a Net: Human Attempts to Describe the Sacred.* New York: Continuum, 2007.

Wendland, Barbara. *Connections. www.connectionsonline.org.*

————. and Larry Easterling. *Spiritual Family Trees: Finding Your Faith Community's Roots.* Herndon, VA: The Alban Institute, 2001.

Index

Scriptures:

Genesis 41:1-36 10
Genesis 28:10-17 10
Genesis 28:16 21
Exodus 3:1-5 22
Exodus 13:21-22 22
Leviticus 18:22 61
Leviticus 19:19 61
Isaiah 6:8 6
Isaiah 53:2-3 124
Matthew 2:13 11
Matthew 5:11 80
Matthew 6:6 145
Matthew 13:27-30 52
Matthew 15:1-3 129
Matthew 21:31 52

Mark 3:1-4 14
Mark 9:40 52
Mark 10:27 62
Luke 3:11 11
Luke 14:26-27 81
John 10:10 157
John 10:16 52
Acts 2:1-4 22
Acts 5:19-20 36
Acts 5:29 81
Romans 12:2 80
Romans 12:6 68
1 Corinthians 13:11 22
Ephesians 4:15 99
Hebrews 6:1 75